MODERN JAPANESE

An Advanced Reader

Gen Itasaka
Seiichi Makino
Kikuko Yamashita

VOLUME II
Vocabulary and Notes

KODANSHA INTERNATIONAL
Tokyo and New York

Distributed in the United States by Kodansha International/USA Ltd., 114 Fifth Avenue, New York, New York 10011.

Published by Kodansha International Ltd., 2-2, Otowa 1-chome, Bunkyo-ku, Tokyo 112 and Kodansha International/USA Ltd., 114 Fifth Avenue, New York, New York 10011. Printed in Japan.

LCC 73-89698
ISBN 0-87011-222-8
ISBN 4-7700-0426-5 (in Japan)

First edition, 1974
Sixth printing, 1989

目次

Abbreviations

adj. = adjective

adv. = abverb

colloq. = colloquial

conj. = conjunction

N = noun

neg. = negative

S = sentence

(……百までの数がろくろく勘定できないというようなことでは
S
……) p. 5, l. 8 ~ 9

V-masu = stem derived from -masu form of a verb

e. g., kaki-(masu), tabe-(masu)

(……考えがちだ) p. 1, l. 3
V-masu

V-te = stem derived from continuative form of a verb

e. g., kai-(te), tabe-(te), yon-(de)

(……文化哲学の影響を受けて、……) p. 1, l. 2
V-te

Vpr = present (dictionary) form of a verb

e. g., kaku, taberu

(……「賛成である」というところを……) p. 13, l. 16~17
Vpr

Vpt = past form of a verb

(……に聞いたところ、……) p. 4, l. 15~16
Vpt

1　イモ洗いとムギ拾い

〔p. 1〕

1	イモ	potato, sweet potato
	ムギ	grain, barley, wheat
2	ふつう(普通)	in general
	～というと	when one talks about～
	ドイツ流(りゅう)	German school. *cf.* -流, style
	人間精神(にんげんせいしん)	human nature
3	創造的産物(そうぞうてきさんぶつ)	creative outcome (*or* product)
	～といった	such as, like
	次元(じげん)	level, dimension, grade
	～がちだ	[with V-masu] be apt to, be prone to
4	基礎的(きそてき)	fundamental, basic
	より	*adv.*, more. *cf.* [with *adj.*, *adv.*] より大きい, bigger
	機能的(きのうてき)	functional, useful, practical
5	～ではないだろうか	won't it be
6	みずから	by oneself [animate]. *cf.* おのずから, by itself [inanimate]
	創(つく)る	create
	個体(こたい)	individual
	分有(ぶんゆう)する	share
7	伝承(でんしょう)する	transmit, hand down
8	とらえる(捕える)	grasp, perceive
9	当然(とうぜん)～はずだ	should naturally be～

〔p. 1〕

9	ただ	however, but
10	～きる	[with V-masu, do in such a definite way that there is no ambiguity] do definitely
	固定観念(こていかんねん)	fixed (*or* established) idea
	ひっかかる(引っ掛る)	be caught, be implicated, be entangled
11	誤解(ごかい)する	misunderstand
	行動(こうどう)	action, behavior
12	～いく	[with V-te] from now on
13	ニホンザル	Japanese monkeys
	幸島(こうじま)	place-name, an island off the southern coast of Kyushu
14	群(む)れ	group [description of any group of animate objects, e.g., herd, flock, covey, . . .]
	ひょっと	by chance
	1歳半(いっさいはん)	one and a half years old
15	メスザル	female monkeys. *cf.* メス [only for animals, insects, . . .], おんな [for 'women']
	つく	stick to
16	しだいに	gradually
17	伝播(でんぱ)する	propagate, spread
19	注目(ちゅうもく)する	observe

〔p. 2〕

1	血縁(けつえん)	blood (*or* direct) relation
2	チャンネル	channel

〔p. 2〕

3	弾力性	flexibility
4	ルート	route
5	～あたり	about
	～くる	[with V-te] come to～
8	親しむ	be familiar with, be always with. ～に(と)親しむ
	～にもなると	[time limitation for some process (identified by the main predicate)] when one reaches. *cf.* ともなると
	世代	generation
10	～のそれは	それ＝伝播様式 [the demonstrative pronoun それ is usually omitted in colloquial speech because of the pronominal function of の, e.g., ～のは]
	まさに	exactly
13	初期	early stage
14	まるで	completely, utterly
	たわし	scrubbing brush
	こする	rub, scrub, scrape
	みごとに(見事に)	admirably, skillfully
15	後期	later period, later on
	ひと口	one bite
	かじる	bite
	～ては～する	[each time one performs an action (identified by V-te は), one performs another accom-

〔p. 2〕

		panying action (identified by V-masu)] each time one～, one does～
16	つける(漬ける)	dip in
	どうやら	somehow
	塩味	taste of salt, salty
18	味つけ	seasoning. *cf.* 味をつける, give flavor, season
19	砂金採集法	panning method, screening method
20	まく(撒く)	scatter
	砂まみれ	sandy. *cf.* まみれる, be smeared
21	めりこむ	sink into (the ground), cave in
22	非能率的	inefficient. 非-, neg. prefix
	砂ごと	together with sand. -ごと, (together) with, and all
	かきよせる	rake up, rake together
23	海辺	water's edge, coast, seashore
	投げすてる	throw away

〔p. 3〕

2	選鉱法	separation method (of mining)
3	創始者	originator
4	つぎつぎと	one after another
6	オトナ	adult
	保守的	conservative
7	ゆかい(愉快)	delightful, cheerful, fascinating
	メスガシラ	boss she-monkey
	エバ	Eve [here a proper name of a

〔p. 3〕

		monkey]
8	長女（ちょうじょ）	oldest daughter
	サンゴ	Sango [coral, here a proper name of a monkey]
9	利用（りよう）する	use, utilize
10	少女（しょうじょ）	girl, elementary school girl
	じっと見（み）る	stare
11	〜やいなや	＝〜とすぐに, as soon as
12	攻撃（こうげき）	attack
	追（お）いはらう	drive away
	浅瀬（あさせ）	shallows
	よこどりする（横取りする）	usurp, snatch
13	搾取（さくしゅ）	exploitation
	起源（きげん）	origin
	くっつける	attach, link. 〜に(と)くっつける
14	意味深（いみぶか）い	very meaningful, of great significance
15	労（ろう）せずして	without laboring. -ず-, neg. particle
16	これに類（るい）する	this type of
19	身（み）につける	become familiar with
21	思（おも）えば〜である	when one thinks about it, it is〜
22	今西（いまにし）　錦司（きんじ）	1902–, 科学史, 科学評論, 自然史学, 生態学. 岐阜（ぎふ）大学学長.

2 後進国援助の特効薬三つ

〔p. 4〕

1	後進国(こうしんこく)	underdeveloped country
	援助(えんじょ)	aid
	特効薬(とっこうやく)	special virtue, special medicine
2	農地改革(のうちかいかく)	(agricultural) land reform
	断行(だんこう)	carrying out, effecting. *cf.* ～する, carry out (resolutely)
3	一括(いっかつ)する	look at things as a whole, make things into a bundle
4	それぞれ	respectively
	事情(じじょう)	circumstances, conditions
	異(こと)なる	differ
5	近代化(きんだいか)のために，ということで	in terms of "for (the sake of) modernization"
	総括(そうかつ)する	summarize
6	結局(けっきょく)	in the long run, in the final analysis, after all
	帰(き)する	come to, result in. に～
	～のではないか	[rhetorical question] probably. *literally*, I wonder if it is not that. *cf.* 田中さんは今日は来ないのではないか. Mr. Tanaka probably won't come today. 田中さんは今日は来るのではないか. Mr. Tanaka probably

〔p. 4〕

		will come today.
7	解放（かいほう）	liberation
	うまくいく	succeed, it goes well
8	台湾（たいわん）	Taiwan
	朝鮮（ちょうせん）	Korea [pre-World War II name of North and South Korea]
	王様（おうさま）	king
9	先頭（せんとう）	the head, front
	やってのける	carry through (without any hesitation)
11	庄園（しょうえん）	manor
	ビルタ	Pakistani land system
	廃止（はいし）	abolition, repeal
	議決（ぎけつ）する	resolve (in congress), decide
	貴族（きぞく）	nobility
12	まき返（かえ）す	roll back, repudiate
	クーデター	coup d'etat
	首相（しゅしょう）	prime minister
	牢（ろう）につなぐ	throw into jail
13	国王親政（こくおうしんせい）	direct imperial rule
	やはり	all the same, still, nevertheless
	向（む）かう	tend to, head for
14	逆行（ぎゃっこう）する	move backward
15	～ところ	＝～ら [with Vpt, the conjunction indicates that what follows is a result of the action identified by Vpt] when, as

〔p. 4〕

15	演説(えんぜつ)	(public) speech, lecture
	筋(すじ)	line, plot (of a play). *literally*, muscle
17	それもそのはずです	*idiom*, no wonder
	単(たん)に	simply
18	実施(じっし)	enforcement, execution. *cf.* ～する, carry into effect, put (a system) into operation
	ゆがめる	distort, warp
	現状(げんじょう)	present conditions

〔p. 5〕

1	食料(しょくりょう)	food, provisions
	状態(じょうたい)	situation
	～というか	[when one has not expressed an idea as intended, one uses というか immediately after the unsuitable word and rephrases the idea] or rather I should say
	栄養(えいよう)	nutrition
2	やる気(き)	motivation, desire
3	資本主義(しほんしゅぎ)	capitalism
4	社会主義(しゃかいしゅぎ)	socialism
	差(さ)	difference
5	政情(せいじょう)	political situation
	うらなう(占なう)	forecast, tell a fortune
6	共通(きょうつう)の	common
7	普及(ふきゅう)	spread, popularization

〔p. 5〕

8	民衆(みんしゅう)	people, masses
	ろくろく	＝ろくに, sufficiently [with neg]
	勘定(かんじょう)	calculation, computation
9	〜というようなことでは	S_1〜S_2 [one draws an explicitly or implicitly negative conclusion(S_2) from S_1 which is usually of negative nature] if it is the case that〜, then 〜
	はなはだ	＝たいへん, very
10	せい	＝ため, because of, due to
	給料(きゅうりょう)	salary, wages
11	計算(けいさん)	calculation, accounts
12	連中(れんちゅう)	party, company, set, people
	支払分(しはらいぶん)	share, payment
	ごまかす	cheat
	チップ	tip
13	渡す(わたす)	hand, deliver
	喜ぶ(よろこぶ)	be glad, be pleased
	考えこまされる(かんがえこまされる)	it makes one ponder. *cf.* 考えこむ, ponder. 考えこませる, make someone ponder
15	抱える(かかえる)	employ, keep, hold in one's arms
16	生産(せいさん)	production
	増加(ぞうか)	increase
17	方式(ほうしき)	form, mode, method
	バース・コントロール	birth control

〔p. 5〕

18	条件(じょうけん)づける	put conditions on～
	指導者(しどうしゃ)	leader
19	単(たん)なる	*literary*, ＝ただの, only mere, simple, sheer
	幻覚(げんかく)	illusion, hallucination
20	そこのところ	that point, that part
	サゼスション	suggestion
21	普通教育(ふつうきょういく)	average (*or* basic) education
22	～率(りつ)	rate

〔p. 6〕

1	篤農家(とくのうか)	conscientious farmer
	続出(ぞくしゅつ)する	appear one after another, crop up
	稲(いね)	paddy, a rice plant
	品種(ひんしゅ)	(plant) breeding, variety, breed
2	神力(じんりき)	proper name of a rice species
	愛国(あいこく)	proper name of a rice species
	つくり上(あ)げる	develop
	試験場(しけんじょう)	laboratory
3	交配(こうはい)する	crossbreed, cross-fertilize
5	出現(しゅつげん)	appearance, emersion
	背後(はいご)	the back. ～には, behind
8	どうも	＝いかにも, indeed, certainly
	増産(ぞうさん)	increasing production. *cf.* ～する, increase production
9	～みたい	*colloq.*, ＝～のような
	～はおろか	let alone, to say nothing of, not to mention

〔p. 6〕

10	接触（せつしょく）	contact, touch
	にぶい	dull, scarce
13	どれほど	how (much, many, etc.), to what extent
14	長期的（ちょうきてき）	long-term, long-range
	運命（うんめい）	fate, future, destiny
	予測（よそく）	estimation, forecast
	確信（かくしん）する	be convinced of ～, be sure of～
16	外資（がいし）	＝外国資本（がいこくしほん）, foreign capital
	導入（どうにゅう）	introduction, importation
	推進（すいしん）	propulsion. *cf.* ～する, propel, promote
17	味（あじ）わう	taste, experience
	苦（にが）い	bitter, unpleasant
18	ラテンアメリカ	Latin America
19	被害（ひがい）	damage, injury
	はなはだしい	extreme, excessive
	～を初（はじ）めとして	not to mention～
20	つぶす（潰す）	crush, smash
	いくらでも	countless, ever so many
21	そろって	altogether
	逃（に）げ出（だ）す	slip away

〔p. 7〕

1	誘致（ゆうち）	inducement, attraction. *cf.* ～する, invite, attract
	置（お）きかえる	replace, change
2	大会社（だいがいしゃ）	big company

〔p. 7〕

2	地方各府県（ちほうかくふけん）	every local district
	知事（ちじ）	prefectural governor
3	総務部長（そうむぶちょう）	general affairs director
	地元（じもと）に	in that locality
5	経営能力（けいえいのうりょく）	managerial ability
	たよる	rely on
	規制（きせい）	prescription, regulation, control
	調節（ちょうせつ）	regulation. *cf.* 〜する, regulate, adjust
7	役割（やくわり）	role. 役割を果（は）たす, play a role
12	〜にもかかわらず	despite the fact that, inspite of
	これからは	from now on, in the future
15	万能薬（ばんのうやく）	cure-all
	100余国（ひゃくよこく）	over one hundred countries. -余-, over
16	当（あ）てはめる	apply
	伸（の）びる	extend, stretch, grow
18	中尾（なかお）　佐助（さすけ）	1916–, 植物学, 農学, 大阪府立（ふりつ）大学教授

3　話しことばにおける日本人の論理

〔p. 8〕

1	論理(ろんり)	logic
2	相手(あいて)	person with whom one is dealing, listener, the other person
	相手中心(あいてちゅうしん)	thinking of the other person, understanding an opponent's point of view. *cf.* 自己中心, self-centered
3	～ということになる	come to mean, it boils down to
	対人関係(たいじんかんけい)	personal relationship, human relationship
4	社交(しゃこう)	social contact, social life
	初歩的(しょほてき)	elementary
5	原則(げんそく)	principle
	理想的(りそうてき)	ideal
	常に(つねに)	usually
6	顔色(かおいろ)	a look, facial expression
	センテンス	sentence
	肯定(こうてい)	affirmative
7	結ぶ(むすぶ)	tie, end, finish
	否定(ひてい)	negative
	疑問(ぎもん)	interrogative
	～形(けい)	type, form
8	とことん〔まで〕	*colloq.*, to the finish

〔p. 8〕

8	この際(さい)	at present
9	大鵬(たいほう)	Taihō, Grand Champion of Sumo (Japanese wrestling), 1961–1971
	退陣(たいじん)する	retire
	～してもらいたい	I want him to (retire)
10	言(い)いたいところだった	one was on the verge of saying. *literally*, one was at the point of wanting to say
	いかにも	really, very much
	ファン	fan, admirer
11	文末(ぶんまつ)	end of a sentence
	～ものですね	[emphatic expression of sincere feeling] honestly
	主旨(しゅし)	purpose
14	すりかえる（すり替える）	change A to B secretly (*or* sneakily)
	悪(わる)くいえば	speaking negatively. *literally*, if speak negatively. *cf.* 良くいえば, speaking favorably
	自主性(じしゅせい)	independence
15	オピニオン	opinion
16	通(とお)す	carry out. オピニオンを通す, make one's opinion known
17	イエス	yes
	ノウ	no
	イズ	is
18	イズ・ノット	is not

	〔p. 8〕	
19	はじめて	for the first time
	〔p. 9〕	
1	文頭	beginning of a sentence
	疑問代名詞	interrogative pronoun
2	主語	subject
	述語	predicate
	転倒する	invert
	ハッキリする	become clear
3	こういう	such
	文法	grammar
4	先に	before
	祖先	ancestor
6	封建性	feudalism
7	成り立つ	it can be thought, be realized, be concluded, hold good, consist of
	上位	superior rank in terms of social position. *cf.* 下位
	うかがう	watch, spy upon
8	ムニャムニャと	with a mumble [onomatopoeic word]
9	語尾	word ending
	にごす	use an ambiguous expression
	しいたげる	oppress
	自己防衛	self-defense
10	いちがいに	unconditionally [with neg.]. いちがいにそうともいえない. We cannot absolutely say so.

〔p. 9〕

11	立場(たちば)	situation
12	逆転(ぎゃくてん)する	turn, be reversed
	しばしば	＝たびたび, often
13	金田一(きんだいち)　春彦(はるひこ)	1913–, 国語学(こくごがく)
	大岡政談天一坊(おおおかせいだんてんいちぼう)の巻(まき)	book title, *The Ten'ichibō Volume of the Ōoka Political Episode*
14	おられる	*honorific*, ＝いる
	将軍(しょうぐん)	general
	吉宗(よしむね)	＝徳川(とくがわ)吉宗, Tokugawa Shogun Yoshimune, 1684–1751
	大岡越前守(おおおかえちぜんのかみ)	Governor Ōoka of Echizen, 1677–1751. -守, lord, governor. 越前, place-name
	功(こう)	merit
	賞(しょう)する	honor, award
	松平伊豆守(まつだいらいずのかみ)	Governor Matsudaira of Izu, 1596–1662
15	以下(いか)	Matsudaira and his followers
	幕閣(ばっかく)	staff of the shogunate council
	ウム	yes [from a lord to his followers]
	よう	＝よく
	調(しら)べが届(とど)く	make a thorough investigation
	その方(ほう)	you [from a lord to his followers]
16	なくば	*literary*, ＝なければ, if you weren't around
	天下(てんか)	the whole country, the realm

〔p. 9〕

16	一大事（いちだいじ）	serious matter
	及（およ）ぶところ	it would have become (serious)
	幸（さいわい）に	luckily
	のがれし	*literary,* ＝のがれた, avoided, escaped
17	あっぱれな	splendid, admirable
	はじめ	starting
	城代（じょうだい）	deputy governor of a castle
	所司代（しょしだい）	vice-governor, secretary
	老中（ろうじゅう）	councilor
18	一同（いちどう）	all of you [from a lord to his followers]
	心（こころ）づいた	*literary,* ＝気（き）のついた, sensible
	儀（ぎ）	*literary,* ＝こと
20	身（み）にかかわる	endanger one's life (honor, reputation)
22	事情（じじょう）	incident, situation, actual situation
	相手方（あいてがた）	person with whom one is dealing
	尊重（そんちょう）する	respect

〔p. 10〕

1	しきりに	often, continually
2	提出（ていしゅつ）する	present, propose
	レアード	Laird, Melvin R.
3	傷（きず）つける	hurt, disgrace
4	力説（りきせつ）する	emphasize, put stress on, accentuate

〔p. 10〕

5	やかましく	loudly, often
6	自己中心的（じこちゅうしんてき）	self-centered
	横行（おうこう）する	stride, be at large, be rampant
7	文法（ぶんぽう）のうえから	from the point of grammar, in its grammatical construction
8	まことに	*literary*, ＝ほんとうに, indeed
9	あいまい	ambiguous, evasive
	優（すぐ）れる	be superior to
	国民性（こくみんせい）	national trait
11	かばいあう	shield each other, defend
	いつの間（ま）にか	*idiom*, before one is aware, before one knows it
	なれ合（あ）い	intimacy, conspiracy, collusion
12	おおよその	＝大体（だいたい）の, approximate. おおよそのところで, before one goes too far
	妥協（だきょう）する	compromise
13	表現（ひょうげん）をとる	choose (*or* use) an expression
14	なかなか	rather, very
	論理的（ろんりてき）	logical
15	評（ひょう）する	criticize
	～に原因（げんいん）するところが多（おお）い	＝～によるところが多い, owe a great deal to～
16	ナーナー	*colloq.*, ＝ねーねー[easy compromise, understanding]
17	とかく	*adv.*, be apt to, in many cases, often [with neg. or neg. implication]

〔p. 10〕

17	温(あたた)か味(み)	warmth
18	発言(はつげん)する	utter, speak
	角(かど)が立(た)つ	become hard, harsh
19	つい	*adv.*, without realizing, inadvertently
21	明確(めいかく)に	clearly
22	避(さ)ける	avoid

〔p. 11〕

1	使(つか)いたがらない	[V-masu ending ＋ たがる＝want to do, desire] not wanting to use
2	大出(おおいで)　晃(あきら)	1926–, 国語学
	指摘(してき)する	point out
	接続語(せつぞくご)	connective word
3	押(お)しつけがましい	pushy [listener feels somewhat imposed upon]
5	適切(てきせつ)な	suitable
6	故障(こしょう)する	break down
	～から	because
	遅刻(ちこく)する	be late (for). *cf.* ～に～
	あやまる	apologize
7	～とばかりに	only, completely
9	いくらか	to a degree, somehow
10	やわらかい	mild, soft
	因果(いんが)	cause and effect
11	薄(うす)い	weak, thin, scanty. *cf.* 薄める, water down
	～感(かん)じである	*with adj.*＝～感じがする, strike

〔p. 11〕

		one as～
14	前後（ぜんご）	order, sequence
16	そうした	that kind (*or* aspect) of
18	省略（しょうりゃく）する	omit
19	余韻（よいん）	aftereffect
21	やたらに	frequently

〔p. 12〕

3	ポチ	Pochi, proper name of a dog
	ワンワン	bowwow
	ほえる	bark
5	調子（ちょうし）	tones, fashion
6	似（に）たりよったり	be much the same
9	幼稚（ようち）な	immature, childish
10	西洋画（せいようが）	Western-style painting
	カンバス	canvas
	すみずみ	furthest corner, each corner
	色彩（しきさい）	color, paint
	塗（ぬ）りつぶす	paint completely (without leaving any blank space)
11	～に対（たい）し	as opposed to～, in contrast with～
	余白（よはく）	unfilled space, blank
	西欧（せいおう）	Western Europe
12	接続詞（せつぞくし）	conjunction
	関係代名詞（かんけいだいめいし）	relative pronoun
	系統的（けいとうてき）	systematic
	緻密（ちみつ）に	precisely, minutely
14	ときには	sometimes

〔p. 12〕

20	別(わか)れ	farewell, parting, division, offshoot. *cf.* 分(わ)かれる, split
	際(さい)して	when, on occasion
	さよう	*classical,* ＝そう
21	しからば	*classical,* ＝それでは
	これにて	*classical,* ＝これで
	失礼仕(しつれいつかまつ)る	*classical,* ＝失礼いたします, I must be going now, I must say good-bye

〔p. 13〕

1	じゃあネ	see you. *literally,* well, then
	じゃあ、どうしようというのか〔わからない〕	I wonder what they want to do (after saying "ja")
5	非断定(ひだんてい)	indecision, indecisiveness. 非-, neg. prefix
	回避(かいひ)	evasion
9	見本(みほん)	sample
11	柔(やわ)らげる	soften, tone down
13	二重否定(にじゅうひてい)	double negative
16	あらずんばあらずや	*classical,* ＝ないのじゃないか, I wonder if there isn't
	賛成(さんせい)	agreement
17	〜ところを〜	[with Vpr, one could (*or* should) do something (identified by Vpr) but in fact one cannot perform this action due to some circumstance] although one could (*or* should)

〔p. 13〕

17	手ばなしで	openhandedly, openly
20	お座敷小唄	type of ballad [popular at geisha houses]
	一節	one paragraph, phrase, line
	文句	phrase, words

〔p. 14〕

1	高嶺	high peak
	清らかな	clean, pure
2	先斗町	place-name, district in Kyoto, the location of many geisha houses
	下界	this world
	高貴の	noble
3	花柳界	frivolous society
	とける	melt, be loved by a man
8	単純否定	simple negative
11	いったい	in fact, really [with interrogative]
13	おしゃべり	chattering, gossip
14	経済大国	economically strong country
	国会答弁	bureaucratic reply to (*or* defense against) queries of Japanese Diet members
	社説	editorial
15	こうなると	if this is the case
16	～などとはいっていられない	it must not be the occasion for saying
17	曰く	*classical*, ＝言う. *cf.* 孔子曰く,

	〔p. 14〕	
		Confucius says
18	解放戦線（かいほうせんせん）	liberation front
	あながち	necessarily, always [with neg.]
19	戦乱（せんらん）	war, war and tumult
	巻（ま）きこむ	entangle, roll up, enfold
	おそれ	fear. *cf.* おそれる, be fearful of
21	慎重（しんちょう）に	carefully, prudently
	ベトコン	Viet Cong
22	注意深（ちゅういぶか）さ	carefulness
	〔p. 15〕	
1	逃（に）げを打（う）つ	make an escape
2	～とくる	come up to
	病（やまい）こうこうである	*idiom*, the habit is now deeply ingrained, be past mending
3	除外（じょがい）する	make an exception of, exclude
4	れっきとした	legitimate
	インフレ	inflation
5	政府（せいふ）といたしましては	＝政府は, the way the government sees
	現段階（げんだんかい）	present level
6	必（かなら）ずしも～ない	not necessarily [with neg.]
8	～につきましては	＝～については
	対策（たいさく）	countermeasure, adequate measure
	善処（ぜんしょ）する	manage tactfully, make the best of
	所存（しょぞん）	＝つもり, opinion, intention
11	言（い）いまわし	phrasing

〔p. 15〕

12	言いわけ（い）	explanation, defense, excuse
13	言いのがれ（い）	evasive answer, excuse
14	～ぐらいに	＝ほど. *cf.* 彼ほどよく勉強（べんきょう）する学生（がくせい）はいない, There is no student who studies as hard as he.
19	警句（けいく）	adage, witty remark
20	筆者（ひっしゃ）	author, the present writer

〔p. 16〕

2	自身（じしん）	self
	私（わたくし）のことを申（もう）して、なんですが	I don't need to talk about myself but . . .
	自慢話（じまんはなし）	boastful talk. *cf.* 自慢, pride, boasting
	具合（ぐあい）	condition, case, example
4	出席（しゅっせき）する	attend, be present
5	たいがい	*adv.*, generally, often
	取（と）りいそぎ	in haste
6	まとめる	put it together, finish
	検討（けんとう）	examination, investigation
7	母集団（ぼしゅうだん）	population [in statistics], matrix
	完全（かんぜん）サンプル	conclusive sample
8	有意差（ゆういさ）	margin of validity
	検定（けんてい）	approval, inspection, check
10	披露宴（ひろうえん）	wedding banquet
	テーブル・スピーチ	speech, address. *literally*, table-speech
	突然（とつぜん）	on short notice, unexpectedly

〔p. 16〕

10	指名（しめい）	nomination
11	～やら	＝～か [interrogative particle]
12	大家（たいか）	expert, leading figure, authority.
	先輩（せんぱい）	senior
	さしおいて(差し置いて)	leave behind, ignore
	～ごとき	*literary*, ＝～のような, like
	若輩（じゃくはい）	young person
	祝辞（しゅくじ）	formal congratulations
13	～といったぐあいで	and so on and so forth
14	一言（いちごん）	a word
	次第（しだい）	reason, cause
15	長々と（ながなが）	at great length
	豊富（ほうふ）	abundance
19	こと～となると	when it is the case of
	社交上の（しゃこうじょう）	of social etiquette
20	仕事上の（しごとじょう）	of business affairs
	たちまち	immediately
	～嫌い（ぎらい）	dislike
21	男子ことあげせず（だんし）	*idiom*, men shouldn't talk much. *cf.* ことあげ, polemic
	つべこべ	*colloq.*, ＝あれこれ, jabber, chatter
	理屈（りくつ）	reason, logic
	不言実行（ふげんじっこう）	in deed but not in words
23	いさぎよい	brave, manly. *cf.* おとこらしい, manly
	たとえ～としても	even though

〔p. 17〕

1	～がましい	look like, smack of
	いかん	*literary*, ＝どう, 何(なに), what (kind of)
2	問(と)わず	regardless of
3	くずれる	crumble, collapse, get out of shape
4	くどくどと	repeatedly and at great length
5	国鉄(こくてつ)	the Japanese National Railways
6	先(さき)に顔(かお)を出(だ)す	show itself first
7	はばをきかす	have great influence, assert one's own importance
9	堀川(ほりかわ)　直義(なおよし)	1911–, 心理学(しんり), 成城(せいじょう) 大学教授

4 「都市の日本人」を書いた頃のこと

〔p. 18〕

2	駐日(ちゅうにち)	official (*or* accredited) resident in Japan. *cf.* 駐日大使(たいし), ambassador to Japan
	連合王国(れんごうおうこく)	United Kingdom
	使節団(しせつだん)	mission, delegation
	顧問官(こもんかん)	councilor
	無給(むきゅう)の	unsalaried, unpaid
	秘書(ひしょ)	secretary
3	やっと	=ついに, at last, after great difficulty
4	踏(ふ)む	step. 土(つち)を踏む, land, arrive
	実習(じっしゅう)	actual practice, training
	外務省(がいむしょう)	Foreign Office
5	いかめしい	ostentatious, grandiose, high-sounding
	肩書(かたが)き	title
	おかげ	=ため, から, due to, owing to
6	留学(りゅうがく)する	study abroad, go abroad for study
	奨学金(しょうがくきん)	scholarship
	貰(もら)う	receive
7	マッカーサー	MacArthur, Douglas
	総司令部(そうしれいぶ)	General Headquarters
	肝心(かんじん)な	important, vital. *cf.* 肝(きも), liver;

〔p. 18〕

		心(こころ), heart
7	許可(きょか)	permission. ～がおりる, permission is granted
8	～なんぞ	＝～なんか, and like
	御免(ごめん)こうむる	decline, be excused from doing something, beg off
9	珍(めずら)しい	unusual, novel, rare
	慈悲(じひ)	mercy
	発揮(はっき)する	exhibit (power, mercy *or* any abstract object), show
10	擬装(ぎそう)する	disguise, pretend, camouflage
11	経(た)つ	pass, elapse
	さすがの	even [a person or a group who is not noted for this]
12	排斥(はいせき)	rejection, exclusion
	方針(ほうしん)	policy, course
	本来(ほんらい)の	original
13	探(さが)す	search for
14	手(て)がかり	clue, key, connections
	求間(きゅうま)	room wanted
15	2階(にかい)の6畳(ろくじょう)	6-tatami-mat room on a 2nd floor
16	空(あ)く	be vacant
	幸運(こううん)	good fortune
17	見知(みし)らぬ	unfamiliar, unknown, strange. *cf.* 見知る, know by sight
	泊(と)める	put a person up, lodge someone. *cf.* 泊まる, lodge

	〔p. 18〕	
18	よっぽど	*adv.*, really, in fact, by far
	ものずきな(物好きな)	inquisitive, strange, eccentric
	気(き)をつけろ	watch out [imperative]
19	忠告(ちゅうこく)	warning, advice
	〔p. 19〕	
2	弁天(べんてん)さん	Benzaiten, Shinto goddess of fortune
	蓮(はす)	lotus
	復活(ふっかつ)する	revive, be restored
3	不忍(しのばず)の池(いけ)	place-name, a pond in Ueno Park, Tokyo
	ほとり	edge, vicinity
	廻(まわ)る	＝回(まわ)る, make a detour
	下山町(しもやまちょう)	place-name
4	酒屋(さかや)	liquor store
	家並(いえなみ)	a row of houses
	～軒(けん)	counter for 'house'
5	ちゃんと	＝正(ただ)しく, properly
	床(とこ)の間(ま)	ornamental alcove where Japanese place *kakejiku* (hanging scroll) and flowers
8	物置(ものお)き	storehouse
9	路地(ろじ)	alley
	へだてて	*adv.*, beyond, across
	向(む)かいの家(いえ)	the house across the street
	内職(ないしょく)	side job
10	ガチャンガチャン	bang-bang [onomatopoeic word]

〔p. 19〕

10	木琴（もっきん）	xylophone
	せせこましい	narrow and crowded
11	密集（みっしゅう）する	jammed in, crowded, packed together
	うようよする	squirm in a swarm, be crowded
12	おかみさん	casual way of saying ‘house-wife,’ wife of another
	井戸端会議（いどばたかいぎ）	back-fence chatter. *literally*, well-side gossip
13	社会学徒（しゃかいがくと）	student of sociology
14	物理的（ぶつりてき）	physical
15	頻度（ひんど）	frequency
	最大化（さいだいか）	maximization
16	山の手（やまのて）	uptown (Tokyo)
	門構え（もんがまえ）	furnished with a gate
17	人柄（ひとがら）	character, personality
	魅力（みりょく）	charm, fascination, appeal
18	～と気（き）があう	hit it off with, get along with
20	ことわっておくが	explaining this further
	別（べつ）に	especially
21	～以上（いじょう）	as long as
22	純粋（じゅんすい）の	pure, genuine
	好奇心（こうきしん）	inquisitiveness, curiosity
	原動力（げんどうりょく）	motivating power

〔p. 20〕

1	大抵（たいてい）の人（ひと）	most people
2	多（おお）かれ少（すく）なかれ	more or less
3	一層（いっそう）	*adv.*, ＝もっと, more

〔p. 20〕

5	もったいぶる	put on airs, assume an air of importance. *adj.*, もったいぶった, pretentious
	用語	terminology
	体系化する	systematize
7	ともかく	let alone, apart from
	少なくとも	at least
8	人のすることなすこと	whatever people do
	面白くてたまらない	[*adj.* て＋たまらない] too interesting to ignore. *literally*, interesting enough not to resist
9	名人	master, expert
	内幕	the inside
10	解釈	explanation, interpretation
	要領	main point, summary. ～を得る, be to the point, hit the mark
11	たてまえ(立て前)	front, principle
	ほんね(本音)	one's true intention
	見抜く	see through
12	そうかと言って	[this idiomatic conjunction is used to deny some expected conclusion that might be drawn from one's preceding remark; the actual conclusion is usually in the negative] but～, however～
	つきもの	something inseparable from, an accessory

〔p. 20〕

12	人の悪さ	malice
13	偉いこと	greatness
	寛大	magnaminity, liberality
	みみっちい	mean, stingy
14	好材料	good data, good material
15	腹をかかえて笑う	burst out laughing
	口実	excuse, pretext
16	隣	next door
	夫婦喧嘩	quarrel between husband and wife
	～して笑えば、～して笑う	[feeling of repetitive action or sometimes parallel action] laugh while ～ing ～, and laugh while ～ing ～
17	へまをやる	botch, make a mess of
	ものを知らない	innocent, unsophisticated
18	たね（種）	source
19	世話好き	obliging, kind
20	使命	＝仕事, duty
22	ややもすれば	at the least
	野蛮人	barbarian, savage
23	先入観	preconception

〔p. 21〕

1	ぼや（小火）	small fire, blaze
2	腕	arm
	つかまえる	grab
	ひっぱる	pull
3	いくら外人の私でも	even the foreigner as I am

〔p. 21〕

		いくら高（たか）くても, no matter how expensive it is
7	いくぶんか	to some degree, certain extent
	訓練（くんれん）	training. ～にあたる, give training, engage in training
8	人（ひと）	＝他人（たにん）, someone, others
	たとえ～でも	even though
9	御馳走（ごちそう）さま	*idiom*, thank you, it was delicious
	だれそれ	such and such a person
10	みがく	polish, brush
	失礼（しつれい）にあたる	＝失礼になる, be impolite
11	葬式（そうしき）	funeral service
	おかえし	return gift
12	値段（ねだん）	price
	算出（さんしゅつ）する	calculate
	様々（さまざま）な	＝いろいろな, various
	規準（きじゅん）	standard
	こまごまと	in detail
14	きつい	strict, stern
	～でも	also
	日記（にっき）	diary
	元旦（がんたん）	New Year's Day
	どてら	cotton-lined winter kimono worn by men
15	やりとり	exchange
16	風呂（ふろ）	bath
17	夕（ゆう）べ	last night

	〔p. 21〕	
19	おめでとう	*idiom*, Happy New Year!, Congratulations!
22	～くらいだから	so that
	〔p. 22〕	
1	ひろめる	expand, broaden
2	八百屋（やおや）	greengrocery
	ぼんぼり	lamp, lantern. ～をたく, light a lamp
3	茶席（ちやせき）	occasion for a tea ceremony
	～ってさ	*colloq.*, ＝～ということです
5	通夜（つうや）	a wake
7	～に深入（ふかい）りする	go deep into, get involved in
9	漠然（ばくぜん）とした	vague
10	野心的（やしんてき）な	ambitious
	転（てん）じる	turn, alter, shift
	町会長（ちようかいちよう）	mayor of a town assembly
11	理事（りじ）	director, trustee
	好人物（こうじんぶつ）	good-natured
12	快（こころよ）く	pleasantly, agreeably
	相談（そうだん）	counseling ～にのる, give advice
	便宜（べんぎ）	convenience. ～をはかる, accommodate
13	ことわる	refuse
14	苦笑（くしよう）する	force a smile
15	やりて（やり手）	operator
	男（おとこ）まさり	woman of masculine spirit
17	ドーア	1925–, Dore, Ronald P. 社会学（しやかい）

5　母の話

〔p. 23〕

1	母の話（ははのはなし）	a newspaper column, "What My Mother Told Me"
2	華道（かどう）	＝生け花（いけばな）, the art of flower arrangement
	～というからには	[with N or S, one expects something or someone (identified by N) to have a specific, positive quality] if there is such a thing as～
	こもる	be filled with, be permeated with
4	活花（いけばな）	＝活け花
6	天地人（てんちじん）	rules of flower arrangement. *literally*, heaven, earth and man
	真行草（しんぎょうそう）	style of flower arrangement. 真＝正格（せいかく）; right, 草＝modification with elegance; 行＝in between 真 and 草
7	やかましい	fastidious, bothersome
	約束（やくそく）	convention, pledge, promise
	形式主義（けいしきしゅぎ）	formalism
8	大きに（おおきに）	＝大いに, greatly, very
10	飾る（かざる）	decorate
	主人（しゅじん）	master, dominant figure

〔p. 23〕

10	何(なん)といっても	*literally*, no matter what one says
	掛軸(かけじく)	hanging scroll
11	引立(ひきた)たせる	emphasize, bring out
	生(い)きる	be striking, live
12	働(はたら)き	function, purpose
13	活(い)ける	arrange flowers
	～も～次第(しだい)	whatever one arranges depends on～
	牡丹(ぼたん)	tree peony, Chinese peony
14	画軸(がじく)	hanging scroll with a picture
	芍薬(しゃくやく)	(herbaceous) peony
	～たりしたら	＝～たりなどしたら, if one does such things as～
	不即(ふそく)にして不離(ふり)	neutral, non-committal
15	松柏(しょうはく)何(なん)とかにして濃(こ)し	*proverb*, to be as consistently virtuous as the evergreen is forever green
16	水仙(すいせん)	daffodil
	つつましく	modestly, humbly
17	横物(よこもの)	scroll hung horizontally
	相応(そうおう)する	fit, suit
	工夫(くふう)	scheme, means
18	いわれてみれば	if told
	成程(なるほど)	indeed
19	内助(ないじょ)の功(こう)	wife's assistance, help from a partner (*or* assistant)
	折柄(おりから)	＝ちょうど今(いま), just now (*or* then)

	〔p. 23〕	
19	婦人週間（ふじんしゅうかん）	Women's Week
	〔p. 24〕	
1	時代（じだい）おくれ	out of date
2	たしなみ	accomplishments in arts, music, way of life etc.
3	細君（さいくん）	wife [used among male friends]
	先（さき）きに立（た）つ	stand in front
	目（め）につく	make oneself noticed, draw attention
4	これ	[the demonstrative pronoun これ refers to the preceding sentence: 主人より . . . 賞められなかった]
5	そのもの	itself
	それ自身（じしん）	its own
7	あくまで	to the utmost (*or* last degree)
9	いかなる	＝どんな
	自我（じが）	self, ego
10	同調（どうちょう）させる	agree with, match
11	何（なに）も知（し）るところはない	something I don't know anything about, it's none of my business
12	漫画（まんが）	comics
	ブロンディ	Blondie
	～といい～といい	for example
	マギィ	Maggie
13	奔放自由（ほんぽうじゆう）な	wild, free
	生（い）きのいい	lively, fresh

〔p. 24〕

13	～ごとく	＝～ように
14	在る（あ）	be
	念願する（ねんがん）	desire earnestly
	どこへ置かれようとも（お）	no matter where N is put
15	ゆがめる（歪める）	distort, bend
	墓場（はかば）	graveyard
16	幸福（こうふく）	happiness, welfare
	～に相違ない（そうい）	＝～にちがいない
17	あの	that (specific)
	ダグウッド	Dagwood
	ジグス	Jiggs
19	復活させる（ふっかつ）	revive
20	現に（げん）	＝実際に（じっさい）, actually
	新家庭（しんかてい）	newlyweds
	いずれも	all
21	順応する（じゅんのう）	adapt
	別人（べつじん）	different person, new person

〔p. 25〕

1	ふたたび	once again
3	出来上りの一歩手前（できあがり、いっぽてまえ）	one step before fully blooming (*or* completion)
5	余地（よち）	margin, space, room
	任せる（まか）	leave N to. *cf.* ～に～を任せる, leave (something) to (a person)
6	迎える（むか）	welcome, receive
7	時刻（じこく）	moment, time
	絶頂（ぜっちょう）	peak, summit

〔p. 25〕

7	勢（いきおい）	strength, influence
8	間（ま）の抜（ぬ）けた	unbalanced space. *literally*, stupid, dull. *cf.* 間の抜けた人（ひと）, stupid person
	すき間（ま）	gap, crevice
10	突放（つきはな）し	throwing, *cf.* 突き放す, throw off, cast off, desert
11	覚束（おぼつか）ない	be unreliable, be questionable. *cf.* 成功（せいこう）は〜, the success is questionable
	藤（ふじ）	wisteria
	〜なら	for example
12	日（ひ）ごろから	＝いつも, always
	自然観察（しぜんかんさつ）	observation (*or* view) of nature
13	編集（へんしゅう）	collection, editing
14	大（おお）げさな	exaggerated, pretentious
15	活（い）け手（て）	person arranging flowers. 手＝人 [suffix]
	呼吸（こきゅう）	breathing, life
	合致（がっち）する	agree
16	たかが〜などといい切（き）れたことではない	it's something more than〜. *literally*, it's not something like saying for sure that it's only〜
17	事実（じじつ）	*adv.*, in fact
	当座（とうざ）	＝その時（とき）, at the time
	物足（ものた）りない	be unsatisfactory, feel something lacking

	〔p. 25〕	
17	～あたりになれば	＝～ぐらいになれば
18	整(ととの)える	arrange, complete arrangements
	つぼみ	bud
19	枝頭一点(しとういってん)の光彩(こうさい)	a point of brilliance at the end of the branch
20	アクサン	accent [from French]. *cf.* アクセント
	ぐっと	firmly, very much
	引緊(ひきしま)る	be pulled together, be compact
	合点(がてん)する	comprehend, understand
22	性急(せいきゅう)な	impatient, short-tempered
23	即座主義(そくざしゅぎ)	belief in ready-made articles
	通用(つうよう)する	pass, be current
	〔p. 26〕	
3	～かぎりには	＝～以上(いじょう)は, as long as～
4	成行(なりゆ)き	developments, progress, outcome
	謙虚(けんきょ)な	modest, humble, subtle
5	～のゆえに（由，故）	because of～
	天真(てんしん)の	genuine, innocent
	清潔(せいけつ)な	pure, clean
6	奥深(おくぶか)い	deep, profound
7	もはや	＝もう, not any more [with neg.]
	歓迎(かんげい)する	welcome
8	極(きわ)める	go to the end, attain, reach
9	衰(おとろ)える	decrease, decline

〔p. 26〕

9	順(じゅん)	process, stage, order
	躊躇(ちゅうちょ)	hesitation
10	取捨(とりす)てる	throw away
	鑑賞(かんしょう)に堪(た)える	be appreciated, be worthwhile
11	～たびに	each time
12	さらさせる	make it expose ～. *cf.* さらす, expose
	情(じょう)なし	cruel, inconsiderate
	心得(こころえ)	＝規則, rules, directions
14	何(なに)もかも	everything and anything
	不向(ふむ)きな	unfit for, unsuitable. ～に不向きな
	あるいは	it's not likely but may be
15	喝采(かっさい)する	applause
	公約(こうやく)	(public) pledge, commitment
16	風向(かざむ)き	situation, wind direction
	～次第(しだい)で	depending on
	さっさと	quickly and completely
	思(おも)いきりのよさ	quick determination, swift decision
19	高田(たかだ) 保(たもつ)	1895–1952, 随筆家(ずいひつか)

6　教育熱心

〔p. 27〕

2	幼稚園（ようちえん）	kindergarten
	遠大（えんだい）な	long-range
	実行（じっこう）に移（うつ）す	put into practice
3	区立（くりつ）	administrated by the ward. *cf.* 市（し）立中学校, city junior high school; 私（し）立小学校, private primary school
	番町（ばんちょう）	place-name, a district in Tokyo
4	1時間近（いちじかんちか）く	approximately (*or* nearly) one hour
	園児（えんじ）	kindergartener
	いや	*adv.*, no, rather
	父兄（ふけい）	parents, guardians
5	手（て）ぬるい	mild, lenient, slow
6	わき目（め）もふらずに	keeping one's eyes riveted, apply oneself closely. *literally*, without looking aside
8	役所（やくしょ）	town hall
	出張所（しゅっちょうしょ）	branch office
	管内（かんない）	within the jurisdiction (*or* province)
	変動（へんどう）	fluctuation
	落着（おちつ）いた	quiet
9	学齢前（がくれいぜん）	preschool age, under school age

	〔p. 27〕	
9	架空(かくう)の	fictitious
	転入者(てんにゅうしゃ)	new residents. *cf.* 転入する, be transferred, be moved
10	悩(なや)む	feel annoyed, suffer, be afflicted with
	永田町(ながたちょう)	place-name, a district in Tokyo
	麹町(こうじまち)	place-name, a district in Tokyo
11	日比谷(ひびや)	place-name, a district in Tokyo
13	通学(つうがく)	attending school
	区域内(くいきない)	inside the boundary
14	〜どまりである	[maximum word] is at most, does not exceed
15	越(こ)える	cross over, go over
	もぐり	sneaking in unofficially. *literally*, diving. *cf.* もぐりの, unqualified, bogus
18	浪人(ろうにん)	student who has failed in the entrance examination and is preparing for the next year's tests
	含(ふく)める	include
	実績(じっせき)	record of performance, actual results
	誇(ほこ)る	be proud of
19	大量(たいりょう)	a large quantity (*or* number)
	〔p. 28〕	
1	かくて	thus, in this way
2	確実(かくじつ)	certain, sure

〔p. 28〕

2	起点（きてん）	starting point, terminus
3	信者（しんじゃ）	believer
	学区制（がっくせい）	school-district system
	ワクをくぐる	pass through the boundary (*or* limit)
4	無理（むり）のない	sensible, reasonable, natural
5	準用（じゅんよう）する	apply (the law, provisions) correspondingly to
6	兼務（けんむ）する	hold an additional post, serve concurrently as～
	～までが	[by attaching まで to N one can express that even the least expected candidate such as ～ is now engaged in some action or is under the influence of some condition] even
	あおり	influence, impact. *literally*, blast of hot air, by-blow
7	～つつある	[Japanese translation of English present progressive tense] ～ing, to be in the process of
8	名簿（めいぼ）	register, roster, roll. *literally*, list of names (*or* enrollment)
	めくる	turn over pages
9	表（おもて）むき	official appearance, ostensibly
11	内（ない）しょ	unofficial, secret. ～で, *adv.*, unofficially

〔p. 28〕

11	居所（いどころ）	present address
12	届（とど）ける	register
13	いってみれば	＝いうならば, namely that. *literally*, if one says
	二通（ふたとお）り	two kinds of, two ways
	在校生住所録（ざいこうせいじゅうしょろく）	record of enrolled students' addresses
16	公務員（こうむいん）	public servant
	学歴（がくれき）	academic career, (formal) education
17	旧制高女（きゅうせいこうじょ）	former high school (system) for girls
18	居住（きょじゅう）	residence
19	官舎（かんしゃ）	official residence provided by the government
20	年齢（ねんれい）	age
21	大半（たいはん）	the majority
23	要約（ようやく）する	sum up
	若（わか）くして	although (*or* while) young
	相当（そうとう）な	suitable, proper

〔p. 29〕

1	圧倒的（あっとうてき）	overwhelming
2	いずれは	＝そのうちに, sooner or later, in due course, someday
	各界（かくかい）	each field, various circles
	支配（しはい）する	control
	閥（ばつ）	clan, faction
	一族（いちぞく）	the clan

〔p. 29〕

3	特権	privilege
	引継ぐ	succeed (to), take over
4	せめて	at least
	かなえる	fulfill, carry out
5	偏執狂的な	maniac
	念願	one's heart's desire
	幼児	child
6	危険	danger
	吹き飛ばす	blow off
7	誇張	exaggeration, overstatement
8	選挙管理委員	election administration committeeman
9	登録	registration
	職権	authority in a job
	まっ消する	erase
	子弟	sons, children
10	通知	notification, information
	連日	everyday
	談じこむ	plead in protest, protest against (a measure)
12	無視する	disregard, ignore
	父兄側	parents' side (*or* part)
	非	fault
13	非公式の	unofficial
14	どうせ	at any rate
	無理	unreasonable
	承知	acquiescence
15	ハラ(腹)	plan, intention. *literally*, belly

〔p. 29〕

16	～とは何(なに)ごとだ	[with S, used by a superior to an inferior or to an equal when the speaker is angry at the latter for what he has done] it is a terrible thing that you should～
17	色(いろ)をなしてくってかかる	argue. *literally*, argue being flushed with anger
	踏(ふ)みにじる	trample down, ignore
18	乱(みだ)す	abuse
	ほおかむり	ignore. *literally*, hood one's head with a towel
20	寄付(きふ)	contribution
	税金(ぜいきん)がわり	substitute for a tax
21	納(おさ)める	pay (tax)
22	厚(あつ)かましい	impudent, shameless
	タナあげ	ignore. *literally*, put aside on a shelf
23	ひとのこと	＝他(ほか)のひとのこと

〔p. 30〕

1	排他的(はいたてき)	exclusive, excluding others
2	敵(てき)	enemy
4	セリフ	lines [originally of a play; also used for emphasis or to be slightly sarcastic]
	ふん囲気(いき)	atmosphere
6	支配者(しはいしゃ)	administrator, leader
	養成所(ようせいじょ)	training school

〔p. 30〕

6	世間	general public
7	骨身にしみて感じる	feel deep in one's mind
	コース	course
	エゴイズム	egoism
8	～に満ちる	be filled with～
	ますます	more and more
10	試みに	by way of experiment, for trial
13	トウダイ	[東大 is printed in かたかな to simulate a kindergartener's lisping speech]
	～の	[sentence-final particle の (of のです) is a female speech marker but children of both sexes use it; even a male adult can use it when he talks to a child with empathy]
14	無邪気に	innocently
15	つね日ごろ	everyday, constantly
	寝ものがたり	bedtime story
16	ご名答	clever answer, fine answer, right answer

7 政 治 力

〔p. 31〕

1	政治力(せいじりょく)	political influence
2	大臣(だいじん)	cabinet member
	突(つ)っこむ	grill, assail with questions, thrust in
	〜とする	[with S] let's suppose
	すると	＝そうすると, and then
3	たじたじと	staggeringly, flinchingly
	色(いろ)にも出(だ)さず	＝顔(かお)色にも出さないで
	泰然(たいぜん)として	in a self-possessed manner, calmly
4	その場(ば)かぎりの	just for that situation
	切(き)り抜(ぬ)け	cutting one's way out of
	答弁(とうべん)	reply, defense
	あれ	that guy
5	相当(そうとう)なもの	"big shot," quite a person
	この社会(しゃかい)	＝日本
	押(お)しの強(つよ)い	＝押しが強い, pushy, aggressive
7	押(お)し切(き)る	do (regardless of opposition), push one's way through
	人物(じんぶつ)	able man
	〜など	like
8	官僚(かんりょう)	bureaucrat
	近(ちか)づく	be close to, approach

〔p. 31〕

8	気(き)がしない	be in no mood for, do not feel like doing
9	広津(ひろつ)　和郎(かずお)	1891–1968, 小説家(しょうせつか)
10	独特(どくとく)な	unique
	語感(ごかん)	feel of a word
11	反映(はんえい)する	reflect
12	盛(も)りこむ	incorporate, put in
13	～てきた	continually [up to the present]
15	そのまま	as it is
	意識(いしき)	consciousness
17	連想(れんそう)する	be reminded of, associate ～ with～

〔p. 32〕

1	席(せき)	seat, one's place
	丸山(まるやま)　真男(まさお)	1914–, 政治思想史(せいじしそうし)学者
2	ひとりひとり	each of them
	まとめる	summarize, put in order
3	こうである	is the following
4	対立(たいりつ)	opposition
	闘争(とうそう)	fight
	頭(あたま)に浮(う)かぶ	come across one's mind
5	異(こと)なった	different
	利害(りがい)	interests, concerns. *literally*, advantages and disadvantages
	秩序(ちつじょ)づける	discipline, regularize, establish order
6	折衝(せっしょう)	negotiation, parley
	協定(きょうてい)	agreement, pact

〔p. 32〕

6	到着(とうちゃく)	arrive. ～に到着する
7	くだす	pass (judgement), give (definition)
8	定義(ていぎ)	definition
	落(お)ちつく	settle down
9	あてはめる	apply A to B. A を B にあてはめる
	みる	＝かんがえる
12	差支(さしつか)えなかろう	＝かまわないでしょう, it is probably OK. *cf.* 差支える, *literally*, be hindered
14	明白(めいはく)	clear
15	プラス	plus
	マイナス	minus
	価値感情(かちかんじょう)	feeling of worth (*or* value)
16	うらはら(裏腹)	back and front, double-faced
18	評価(ひょうか)	evaluate
19	ケイベツ	disrespect
	いりまじる	be intermingled
21	分析(ぶんせき)	analysis
	つながる	be connected, be related to. ～につながる

〔p. 33〕

2	私的(してき)な利益(りえき)	private interest (*or* profit)
3	パブリック	public
4	概念(がいねん)	concept
7	代表(だいひょう)する	be representative of, typify, stand for

〔p. 33〕

7	独占（どくせん）する	monopolize
9	代弁（だいべん）する	speak for (someone)
10	観念（かんねん）	idea
	植（う）えつける	implant
12	むしろ	but rather
	前提（ぜんてい）	premise, proposition
14	超越（ちょうえつ）する	transcend, stand aloof from
19	解（かい）する	interpret, understand
	まっ向（こう）から	utterly, absolutely. *literally*, right from the front
20	滅私奉公（めっしほうこう）	unselfish devotion to the public
21	そこで	and then
22	無色中立（むしょくちゅうりつ）	(politically) colorless, neutral

〔p. 34〕

2	公式（こうしき）	formula
	山県（やまがた）　有朋（ありとも）	1838–1922, 総理大臣（そうりだいじん）, 1889–1891
	さかんに	often, repeatedly
3	たたきこむ	drum a lesson into. *literally*, hammer in
4	無色透明（むしょくとうめい）	colorless and transparent, clean
5	脈々（みゃくみゃく）と	continuously, in chains
6	階級的利益（かいきゅうてきりえき）	profit for one class
	滅（めっ）する	perish, destroy
	国民的利益（こくみんてきりえき）	profit for the nation
8	術策（じゅっさく）	stratagem, trick
	戦術（せんじゅつ）	tactics, strategy
10	既存（きそん）の	existing
	機構（きこう）	mechanism, structure

	〔p. 34〕	
10	のっかる	＝乗(の)る, get on, take part in, take advantage of
	勢力(せいりょく)	power, influence
11	運用(うんよう)	practical use, application
	行使(こうし)する	exercise, use
	なんとなく	without knowing why, somehow
12	挑戦(ちょうせん)する	challenge
14	公平無私(こうへいむし)	fairness and unselfishness
16	寝業(ねわざ)	secret and sneaky strategy. *originally*, Judo terminology
18	イキサツ	the circumstances
20	なにがしか	some (amount) of
	暗(くら)い影(かげ)	dark (*or* mysterious) shadow
21	ポリティシャン	politician
22	ステイツマン	statesman
	〔p. 35〕	
1	見越(みこ)す	foresee, speculate
	そのときどきの	as the occasion may demand
2	かけ引(ひ)き	maneuvers, tactics
	私利(しり)	personal profit
	追(お)う	pursue, chase, follow
4	磯野(いその)　誠一(せいいち)	1910–, 家族法(かぞくほう), 元(もと)東京教育大学教授
5	手腕(しゅわん)	skill, ability
6	三木(みき)　武吉(ぶきち)	1884–1956, 政治家(せいじか)
	大麻(おおあさ)　唯男(ただお)	1889–1957, 政治家
7	裏(うら)で工作(こうさく)する	maneuver in the back (*or* behind the scenes)

〔p. 35〕

8	たけている（長けている）	be proficient at, be an expert in
9	選ぶ	choose, select
10	獲得	aquisition
11	無倫理性	amoral
12	向い合う	go hand in hand. *literally*, face each other
	キリスト教	Christianity
15	ふたこと目に	all the time. *literally*, at the second word
	持ち出す	introduce (a subject)
21	孝養の義務	obligation of being devoted to one's parents
	項目	clause, item, proviso
22	自民党	＝自由民主党, Liberal–Democratic Party, founded in 1955
	憲法改正案	proposal for constitutional amendment
23	押しつける	force, push
	自立性	independence

〔p. 36〕

2	とうとぶ	value, respect
3	孤高を保つ	be aloof, remain apart from others, stand high in one's own estimation
	清い	clean, pure
4	無関心	indifference
5	こすからい	cunning and mean

〔p. 36〕

5	ゆだねる	entrust (a person) with (a matter). 〜を 〜にゆだねる
8	さらに	more and more. *literally*, still more
9	悪循環（あくじゅんかん）	vicious circle
12	蝋山（ろうやま） 政道（まさみち）	1895–, 政治学, 元お茶（ちゃ）の水（みず）女子大学学長
15	用（もち）いる	use, adopt, employ
18	個人中心（こじんちゅうしん）	centering on the individual
20	本来（ほんらい）からいうと	properly speaking

〔p. 37〕

2	勝手（かつて）に	as one pleases, freely
	〜にほかならない	＝〜にちがいない, be nothing but 〜
	いいかえると	in other words
4	方向（ほうこう）	direction, bearings
	乱用（らんよう）する	use improperly, abuse
8	政略（せいりゃく）	political tactics, game
	伴（ともな）う	accompany
9	〜とはかぎらない	it does not necessarily follow that〜
10	独走（どくそう）	operate automatically, run by itself
11	見失（みうしな）う	lose sight of, miss
14	和気（わき）アイアイ	harmony and peace
16	不可欠（ふかけつ）	indispensability,
	〜にしても	[with V or adj.] granting that〜

〔p. 37〕

17 政治観（せいじかん）	political view point
カール・シュミット	Karl Schmidt
18 マルクス	Marx, Karl
重（おも）くみる	to regard with respect
19 もの	＝考（かんが）え方（かた）
力点（りきてん）	stress

〔p. 38〕

1 おおやけ	public
4 唱（とな）える	sing, chant
～ところで	[with Vpt, roughly the same as ～ても but is usually used in a generic statement and, therefore, the main predicate is non-past] even if
絶滅（ぜつめつ）	eradicate, exterminate
6 こじつける	force the meaning. こじつけて, by a stretch of language
7 そのあげく	in the end, as the final outcome
無制限（むせいげん）	unlimited, unrestricted
流（なが）れこむ	find (its) way into
10 混同（こんどう）する	confuse, mix up
11 おおう	cover, overspread
13 赤（あか）の他人（たにん）	a complete stranger
ムリヤリに（無理矢理に）	forcibly, under pressure
律（りっ）する	measure, judge
14 親（おや）ごころ	parental feeling
親分子分（おやぶんこぶん）	boss and followers
15 義理人情（ぎりにんじょう）	duty and mercy, social obliga-

〔p. 38〕

tion and humaneness

17	支(ささ)える	support
	真(しん)の	genuine

8 満座の中でお笑い下さっても……

〔p. 39〕

3	世間体(せけんてい)	reputation, social appearances
5	営(いとな)む	carry on, conduct
	だのに	＝そうですけれども, however
8	娘(むすめ)	young woman, girl, daughter
9	しつけ	upbringing, discipline (for children), child training
10	お姑(かあ)さん	mother-in-law
	子(こ)どもの守(も)り	taking care of a child, baby-sitting
11	お巡(まわ)りさん	policeman
15	叱(しか)る	scold
	だって	*colloq.*, but
16	親身(しんみ)に	kindly, warmly. 親身に世話(せわ)する, look after (a person) with tenderest care
19	いずれも	both
	身上相談(みのうえそうだん)	consultation about personal affairs

〔p. 40〕

2	排撃(はいげき)する	reject, denounce
3	期待(きたい)	expectation, hope
	阿(おも)ねる	flatter, fawn upon, please
6	それだけのことだろうか	Is this all there is?
7	挙(あ)げる	give (an example)

〔p. 40〕

8	呉服店（ごふくてん）	dry-goods store, fabric shop
	失火（しっか）	accidental fire
	燃（も）える	burn, blaze
	おりからの	at that time, just then
	恒例（こうれい）の	usual, customary
9	着（き）のみ着（き）のままで	with nothing but the clothes they were wearing
10	やっと	barely
	避難（ひなん）	escape, evacuate
	茫然（ぼうぜん）と	absentmindedly, in a daze
11	すすだらけ	covered with soot. -だらけ, full of, filled with, covered with
	気丈夫（きじょうぶ）な	stouthearted, of firm character
	番頭（ばんとう）	manager, head of personnel and business matters in Japanese-style stores
	たどりつく	find one's way to (a place) at length
13	土蔵（どぞう）	earthen (*or* clay) storehouse. *cf.* くら, storehouse
14	目張（めば）りする	seal
15	かねて	previously, in advance
	壁土（かべつち）	clay for the wall
	ぬりこめる	fill in ～with ～. ～を ～でぬりこめる
16	類焼（るいしょう）	a spreading fire
	ふせぐ	prevent, guard against. *cf.* 火をふせぐ, fight a fire

〔p. 40〕

17	火元（ひもと）	origin of a fire
18	顔（かお）むけできない	*idiom*, to be unable to show oneself in public
19	ふり払（はら）う	tear oneself away from
21	灰燼（かいじん）に帰（き）す	be reduced to ashes
22	申（もう）し訳（わけ）が立（た）つ	justify an apology
	表情（ひょうじょう）	facial expression
	浮（う）かべる	express one's feelings (by a facial expression)
	云云（うんぬん）	＝云々, and so forth

〔p. 41〕

1	不文律（ふぶんりつ）	unwritten law, common law
2	浪花（なにわ）	historical name of 大阪（おおさか）
	契約書（けいやくしょ）	contract, written agreement
	但（ただ）し書（が）き	provisory clause
	～を常（つね）とする	*idiom*, make a habit of ～ing
3	違背（いはい）	violation, infringement
	万一（まんいち）	ten thousand to one (chance)
4	そむく	violate, run counter to. ～にそむく
5	うらみ	bitter feeling, grudge, hostility
	宮本（みやもと）　又次（またつぐ）	1907–, 経済学（けいざい）, 大阪大学教授
6	旨（むね）	principle
	罰（ばつ）	punishment
7	面子（めんつ）	face, honor
8	気（き）がねする	be afraid of giving offence
	誤魔化（ごまか）す	cover up, patch up, deceive
14	傲慢（ごうまん）さ	arrogance, insolence, pride

〔p. 41〕

14	所産（しょさん）	product, result
	生活圏（せいかつけん）	the range of a life, sphere of life
15	パターン	pattern
16	禁（きん）ぜられる	＝禁じられる, be forbidden
17	往来（おうらい）	coming and going
19	身分制（みぶんせい）	social stratification, caste
20	接近（せっきん）	access, proximity, intimate relations
	さまたげる(妨げる)	disturb, obstruct
21	整備（せいび）する	consolidate
	しめ上（あ）げる	exercise rigid control
22	度合（どあ）い	degree, extent, rate
	はるかに	by far, far and away

〔p. 42〕

5	親類縁者（しんるいえんじゃ）	blood relatives and their in-laws
6	脱却（だっきゃく）する	shake oneself free from, emerge from
11	自覚（じかく）	consciousness, insight
13	維持（いじ）	support, maintain
	瞬間的（しゅんかんてき）に	in the twinkling of an eye
14	短時間（たんじかん）	short time
	噂（うわさ）	rumor. *proverb*, 人の噂も七十五日. Rumors last no more than 75 days.
15	永遠（えいえん）	eternity, immorality
18	泥棒（どろぼう）	thief
20	スカートをはく	put on a skirt. *cf.* はく [skirt,

〔p. 42〕

pants, shoes . . .], 着(き)る [shirt, jackets, dress . . .]

22　会田(あいだ)　雄次(ゆうじ)　1916–, 西洋近世史(せいようきんせい), 京都大学人文(じんぶん)科学(かがく)研究所教授

9 「なる」の論理

〔p. 43〕

1	～に対(たい)する	toward, concerning
2	状況(じょうきょう)	circumstances
3	姿勢(しせい)	posture, pose
	現世主義(げんせいしゅぎ)	secularism
4	楽観主義(らっかんしゅぎ)	optimism
5	作為(さくい)	(human) act
	バネ	trigger, a spring
	終末論(しゅうまつろん)	eschatology
	大木(おおき)　英夫(ひでお)	1931–, 実業家(じつぎょうか)
6	ユダヤ人(じん)	Jew
	洪水(こうずい)	flood
7	ノアの箱舟(はこぶね)	Noah's ark
	神話(しんわ)	myth
	行為(こうい)	deed, act
8	人為(じんい)	human power, human work
	やがて	in a short time
	崩壊(ほうかい)する	collapse, break, fall down
9	バベルの塔(とう)	tower of Babel
10	予期(よき)する	expect, sense
11	みちびきだす	take out, deduce
13	予定調和(よていちょうわ)	preestablished harmony
14	台風(たいふう)	typhoon
	猛威(もうい)	fury, violence
	さらす	expose

〔p. 43〕

14	元寇（げんこう）	the Mongolian Invasion, 1274 and 1281
	故事（こじ）	historical allusion, origin
15	観念（かんねん）する	be reconciled to, be convinced
	恵（めぐ）み	a favor, benefaction, kindness
	破壊（はかい）	destruction
	双方（そうほう）	both, two
	もたらす	bring
16	とり去（さ）る	leave out, take away, remove
17	まてば海路（かいろ）の日和（ひより）	*proverb*, ＝待（ま）っているといい事（こと）がある. Good things come to those who wait.
19	～のみならず	＝～ばかりでなく
	さからう	run counter to, oppose, act against (the will of)
	～こと、それが～	*literary*, ＝ ～ ことが ～ [the demonstrative pronoun それ which is used cross-referentially for emphasis, refers *back* to the directly preceding S; in ordinary nonemphatic style それ is omitted]

〔p. 44〕

1	つらなる	be related to～. ～につらなる
	素朴（そぼく）な	simple, artless, naive
	信仰（しんこう）	(religious) belief, faith
	えてして	*adv.*, as a general tendency
2	果報（かほう）	luck, fortune

〔p. 44〕

2	ねてまて	take a nap and wait [imperative]
	前首相	former prime minister
3	池田　勇人	1899–1965, 総理大臣, 1960–1964
	日々是好日	＝毎日いい日だ
4	座右	at one's elbow, at hand
	銘	motto
	所得倍増計画	income-doubling plan
6	高度成長	high rate of economic growth
7	見通し	perspective, unobstructed view
	佐藤　栄作	1901–, 総理大臣, 1964–1972
8	ハーマン・カーン	Herman Kahn, American mathematician
9	引用する	quote
11	以降	thereafter, on and after
	なす(成す)	constitute
12	～によって象徴される	be symbolized by ～, be highlighted by ～. *cf.* 象徴する, symbolize
13	自体	＝そのもの, itself
14	発想	conception, way of thinking
15	雑談	chat
	～伝	biography
18	どうやら	*adv.*, with difficulty, barely
20	この話をつかまえる	pick up this topic
22	～だって	＝～もまた, ～でも
	たてば	in, hence
23	ムキになる	unreservedly

〔p. 45〕

1	～と言(い)ってきかない	insist, insist on ～ing
2	証拠(しょうこ)	evidence, proof
	伊藤(いとう)　昌哉(まさや)	1917–, 実業家
4	スタート	start
8	根(ね)づよく巣(す)くった	deep-rooted
9	反応(はんのう)	reaction
	内閣総理大臣官房広報室(ないかくそうりだいじんかんぼうこうほうしつ)	public relations office for the prime minister
11	世論(せろん)	public opinion. -調査(ちょうさ), public opinion survey
	継続(けいぞく)	continuation
12	うきぼりする	emboss, show clearly, bring into relief. *cf.* うきぼり, raised (relief) work
13	くらし向(む)き	living, livelihood
14	設問(せつもん)	question
	例年(れいねん)	every year
16	ないし	or
18	のちに	afterwards
19	一階級(いちかいきゅう)	one class
	上昇(じょうしょう)する	go up
21	4割方(よんわりがた)	about 40%. -方, about
	追(お)いかける	chase, pursue
22	物価(ぶっか)	prices
	欲求(よっきゅう)	want, craving, desire
	高(たか)まり	rising, increase
23	劣悪(れつあく)さ	poor quality, inferiority

〔p. 46〕

2	消滅(しょうめつ)する	be destroyed
	バラ色(いろ)	rosy
3	ショック	shock
4	とげる	accomplish
	奇蹟的(きせきてき)	miraculous
5	オプティミズム	optimism
12	見田(みた)　宗介(そうすけ)	1937–, 社会学, 東京大学助教授
	青年(せいねん)	youth
13	～への期待(きたい)	hope for～
	おりこんでのこと	＝おりこんだ上(うえ)で考(かんが)えたこと. *cf.* おりこむ, weave～ into, put in
14	専(もっぱ)ら	mainly, solely
15	優先(ゆうせん)する	take precedence
	視野(しや)	field of vision
	逸脱(いつだつ)する	deviate, depart from
16	ともあれ	*literary,* ＝ともかく, in any case, anyway
	縮小(しゅくしょう)する	reduce, cut down
17	線香花火的(せんこうはなびてき)	short-lived (like a firecracker)
20	結晶(けっしょう)	crystallization
	テレポール	television poll
21	生活程度(せいかつていど)	standard of living

〔p. 47〕

1	ぞくする(属する)	be counted as
4	異常(いじょう)に	unusually
6	下層(かそう)	lower class
7	～ものの	[with Vpr, at first the situa-

〔p. 47〕

		tion identified by Vpr looks promising but in actuality things will not improve] although ～
9	下落(げらく)する	fall, drop, depreciate
10	驚異的(きょういてき)	miraculous, wonderful
11	前掲(ぜんけい)	ibid., shown above
12	落差(らくさ)	a head, a water level. ～がある, a gap exists
13	悩(なや)み	struggle, anguish, worry
	姿(すがた)を消(け)す	vanish, disappear, hide oneself
	潜入(せんにゅう)する	infiltrate, sneak in, steal in
18	評価(ひょうか)さるべき	＝評価されるべき
	ことわざ（諺）	proverb, adage
21	若干(じゃっかん)	some, a number of, several
22	しょせん	＝結局(けっきょく), after all
23	風土(ふうど)	climate, natural features

〔p. 48〕

2	曲(まが)りなりにも	at any rate, somehow or other, unsatisfactory as it is
3	少(すく)なからざる	＝少なくない＝とても多(おお)い
4	嘲笑(ちょうしょう)する	ridicule
7	御(ぎょ)しやすい	easy to manage (*or* handle)
12	重荷(おもに)	heavy burden, encumbrance
13	苦悩(くのう)	distress
14	もてはやす	treasure
15	未来学(みらいがく)	futurology, study of future conditions

〔p. 48〕

15 投影(とうえい)する — project, cast a reflection

17 貫(つら)ぬく — carry through

18 篠原(しのはら) 一(はじめ) — 1925–, ヨーロッパ政治史, 東京大学法学部教授

10 義理・人情の世界

〔p. 49〕

1	義理（ぎり）	obligation, (a sense of) duty
	人情（にんじょう）	humaneness, sympathy
3	掟（おきて）	rule
4	庶民（しょみん）	the (common) people, the masses
	詳（くわ）しい方々（かたがた）	specialists. *literally*, people who know things in detail
	～上（うえ）で	＝あとで, [with Vpt] after ～ing, after having done
5	歌舞伎（かぶき）	Kabuki, drama with dances dating from the beginning of the Edo period
	浄瑠璃（じょうるり）	Jōruri, ballad-drama dating from the beginning of the Edo period
	好（この）んで	frequently, willingly, by preference
6	扱（あつか）う	deal with
	察（さっ）する	guess, catch on, see, perceive
	恐（おそ）らく	perhaps
	武家時代（ぶけじだい）	the age of military ascendancy, the samurai age
7	君臣（くんしん）、主従（しゅじゅう）	sovereign and subject, master and servant

〔p. 49〕

8	ふさわしい	suitable, becoming
9	イデオロギー	ideology
10	武士道（ぶしどう）	Japanese chivalry, the way of warriors
11	すぐれて	by far, eminently
13	しみ込（こ）む	permeate, sink into, be imbued
14	滅多（めった）に～ない	rarely, seldom
	何（なに）よりの	best, most
17	～だの～だの	[when enumerating typical examples in a rather sloppy way one lists them using だの～だのという. *cf.* や～や]
18	とげとげしい	harsh, stinging. *cf.* とげ, thorn

〔p. 50〕

1	よそ（他所）	other place, unfamiliar place
3	お互（たがい）	each other
4	水臭（みずくさ）い	reserved, distant, lacking in intimacy
7	閉（と）ざす	shut, close, lock
	あてはまる	be applicable. ～にあてはまる
9	親分子分（おやぶん・こぶん）	a boss and his gang
	師弟（してい）	master and disciple
	雇（やと）い主（ぬし）	employer
	雇（やと）い人（にん）	employee
	間柄（あいだがら）	relationship, terms
10	血縁関係（けつえんかんけい）	kinship
	同郷関係（どうきょうかんけい）	personal relationships among

〔p. 50〕

		people from the same province
10	同業関係	fellowship among people in the same profession
	友人関係	friends and fellows, colleagues and associates
	いずれにせよ	＝いずれにしても
11	及ぶ	reach, come up to. 〜に及ぶ
12	普遍的	universal
15	封鎖	blockade
16	帯びる	have, be tinged with
	〜ことは争えません	there is no denying (the fact) that
17	排他性	exclusivity
	縁故者	relative
18	ひいきにする	favor, patronize, support, side with
20	〜といい	＝〜といいながら
	〜がどうの〜がどうのといいながら	[by どうの is understood a stereotyped predicate for the subject; for example, in this context, ある and 悪い are understood predicates for 義理 and 世間体 respectively] saying something like there is an obligation and one's reputation has been injured
21	人中	in public

〔p. 50〕

21	可く候（べく そうろう）	*classical,* ＝してください
22	恥（はじ）はかきすて	disgrace oneself and never look back
23	賤（いや）しき	low, humble
	業（わざ）	＝仕事（しごと）

〔p. 51〕

1	身過（みすぎ）	＝生活（せいかつ）
	名字（みょうじ）	family name
	疵（きず）	flaw, stain
4	鏡（かがみ）	mirror
6	同志（どうし）	like-minded person
	固（かた）い	rigid, solid
	礼儀（れいぎ）	courtesy, manners
7	綺麗好（きれいずき）な	tidy, neat, love of cleanliness
8	公徳心（こうとくしん）	public sense
	香（かんば）しい	sweet-scented, fair, favorable
	評判（ひょうばん）	rumor
11	偶々（たまたま）	by chance
12	淳風美俗（じゅんぷうびぞく）	simple manners and beautiful customs
14	一味徒党（いちみととう）	fellow-conspirators, partisans
21	果（はた）し合（あ）う	carry out mutually. *literally,* accomplish each other
23	見張（みは）る	watch, look

〔p. 52〕

1	文句（もんく）をつける	make a complaint, grumble
2	どうこう	bad. *literally,* this and that
	内心（ないしん）	real inward feeling, one's mind

〔p. 52〕

4　権力（けんりょく）を振（ふる）う　　exercise one's authority

6　飯塚（いいずか）　浩二（こうじ）　　1906–1970, 人文地理学, 元札幌（さっぽろ）大学経済学部教授

11 ふろの効用

	〔p. 53〕	
1	ふろ	bath
	効用(こうよう)	use, effect
2	公衆浴場(こうしゅうよくじょう)	public bath, bathhouse
	鎌倉時代(かまくらじだい)	Kamakura period, 1192–1333
3	欠(か)くべからざる	indispensable, essential
6	由来(ゆらい)する	originate (in), be derived (from)
7	皮膚(ひふ)	skin
9	けがれ	impurity, uncleanliness
10	きよめる	purify, make clean
12	みそぎ	purification ceremony, ceremonial ablution
14	火山帯(かざんたい)	volcanic zone
	温泉(おんせん)	hot spring
	ゆたかに	abundantly, plentifully
15	お湯(ゆ)	hot water
	医療(いりょう)	medical care
17	わかす	boil
	奈良朝(ならちょう)	Nara period, 710–794. *cf.* -朝 dynasty, court
18	大衆(たいしゅう)	the masses, the general public
19	光明皇后(こうみょうこうごう)	Empress Kōmyō, 701–760
	みずから	oneself, in person
	〔p. 54〕	
1	垢(あか)	dirt, filth

〔p. 54〕

3	ローマ	Rome
	西暦前（せいれきぜん）	B.C. *cf.* 西暦, A.D.
4	中桐（なかぎり）　確太郎（かくたろう）	評論家
5	南北朝時代（なんぼくちょうじだい）	Nanboku period, 1336–1392
	町（まち）ぶろ	*archaic*, ＝銭湯, 公衆浴場
6	カギ	key
	銭湯（せんとう）デモクラシー	public-bath democracy
7	娯楽（ごらく）	recreation, amusement, pastime
8	くふうをこらす	think out a device, invent, tax one's ingenuity
9	ハダカ	nakedness
	士農工商（しのうこうしょう）	the classes of warriors, farmers, artisans and tradesmen
10	さりげなく	in a casual way, nonchalantly
12	わずかの	insignificant
13	かりそめの	temporary
	ユートピア	Utopia
14	もうける（設ける）	provide, set up
	将棋（しょうぎ）	Japanese chess. ～をさす, play a game of Japanese chess
15	サービス	service
16	湯女（ゆな）	woman employed at public baths to wash customers and to serve as a prostitute in the Edo period
17	垢（あか）かき女（おんな）	woman employed at public baths to wash customers in

〔p. 54〕

		the Edo period
17	三助(さんすけ)	bathhouse attendant
18	性的(せいてき)な快楽(かいらく)	sexual pleasure

〔p. 55〕

1	権威主義(けんいしゅぎ)	authoritarianism
2	かくれる	hide
3	ときあかす	=説明(せつめい)する, explain, solve
4	式亭(しきてい)　三馬(さんば)	1776–1822, 落語作家(さっか)
	落語(らくご)	story ending in a joke (usually a play on words) told and acted by one person
	浮世風呂(うきよぶろ)	book title, *Public Baths of the Floating World* (Edo period)
	浮世床(うきよどこ)	book title, *Barber Shops of the Floating World* (Edo period)
5	ありうる	possible, probable
7	代用(だいよう)	substitution
	名勝(めいしょう)	scenic spot
	ペンキ絵(え)	painted picture
8	蒸(む)しぶろ	steam bath
	ザクログチ	a low entrance to the bathing room
9	板(いた)	a board, planking
	すきまから	from (*or* through) the small opening
10	かがむ	stoop down
	はいこむ	enter into, creep into
11	湯槽(ゆぶね)	bathtub

〔p. 55〕

11	湯気（ゆげ）	steam, vapor
	たちこめる	envelop, hang over
12	しかけ	gadget, device
13	後世（こうせい）	in later ages
14	くぐる	pass through (*or* under)
15	なごやかな	amiable, peaceful, soothing
16	タイル	tile
17	原型（げんけい）	prototype, model, pattern
19	壁画（へきが）	mural, fresco
	絵（え）はがき	picture postcard
	模写（もしゃ）する	copy, reproduce
20	大正（たいしょう）・昭和（しょうわ）	Taishō period, 1912–1926; Shōwa period, 1926–
21	東北（とうほく）の松島（まつしま）	place-name in the Tōhoku area, Honshū
	山陽（さんよう）の宮島（みやじま）	place-name in the Sanyō area, Honshū
22	風景（ふうけい）	landscape, scenery, view

〔p. 56〕

1	はめつけ	inlay. *cf.* はめる, inlay; つける, attach
5	混浴（こんよく）	mixed bathing
	禁（きん）じる	prohibit, ban
7	屈伏（くつぶく）	submission, surrender
9	共産部落（きょうさんぶらく）	communal settlement
	心境村（しんきょうむら）	place-name
12	20年（にじゅうねん）を経（へ）て	after (the lapse of) 20 years
14	ヘルス・センター	health center

〔p. 56〕

15	ボーリング	bowling
	スキー	skiing
16	施設(しせつ)	equipment, facilities
	カナメ	main point. *literally*, pivot of a fan
18	駅(えき)ビル	station building
20	切(き)れめ	pause, break
21	都心(としん)	center of a city, downtown
22	仕切(しき)り	partition, break, pause

〔p. 57〕

1	生(せい)を生(い)きる	live a life
4	部長(ぶちょう)クラス	managerial class
7	対等(たいとう)	equality, par
8	プライバシー	privacy
9	うちとけた	openhearted, unreserved
12	鶴見(つるみ)　俊輔(しゅんすけ)	1922–, 哲学(てつがく), 記号論(きごうろん), 同志社(どうししゃ)大学教授
	星野(ほしの)　芳郎(よしろう)	1922–, 現代技術史(げんだいぎじゅつし), 技術論, 立命館(りつめいかん)大学経営学部教授

12 チェンバレン著『日本ふうのもの』

〔p. 58〕

1	日本(にほん)ふうの	Japanese-style
4	めくる	turn over. *cf.* ページをめくる, turn the pages of a book
6	読後感(どくごかん)	impression of a book
7	値打(ねう)ち	value, merit
	つめもの	stuffing, padding (to make a respectable volume), filler
	くわえる	add, supply
	見聞(みき)き	＝見聞(けんぶん), observe, experience, see and hear
8	ものごと辞典(じてん)	encyclopedia. *literally*, dictionary of matters
9	先例(せんれい)	previous example, precedent
10	和漢三才図会(わかんさんさいずえ)	book title, an illustrated encyclopedia, publ. 1712
	嬉遊笑覧(きゆうしょうらん)	book title, a collection of essays on Japan and its culture, publ. 1830
11	規模(きぼ)	scale, scope
14	変革(へんかく)	change, reform
	追(お)うて	*literary*, ＝追って, follow, cover
16	位置(いち)	position
17	石井(いしい)　研堂(けんどう)	1865–1943, 編集者(へんしゅうしゃ)
	名著(めいちょ)	masterpiece, great book

〔p. 58〕

17	明治事物起源(めいじじぶつきげん)	book title, *Origin of Things Meiji*
	〜にしても	[the noun preceding にしても is no exception to the statement (identified by the main predicate)] take〜 for example, it also is〜
19	やとわれる	[passive of やとう] be employed

〔p. 59〕

2	ことさらに(殊更に)	deliberately, particularly
3	ふりをする	pretend, pose
	なげく	deplore, sigh
4	議員(ぎいん)	member of parliament
	ヘンリー・ノーマン	Henry Norman
6	軍隊(ぐんたい)	army
	造船所(ぞうせんじょ)	shipyard
7	ふれる	mention, refer to
8	アラジンのランプ	Aladdin's lamp
	パッとあらわれる	appear suddenly (from nowhere)
9	日本(にほん)もの	book about Japan
	効果的(こうかてき)	effective, successful
12	こもる	be implied. こもってもいよう＝こもってもいるだろう
17	耳(みみ)をかたむける	listen to, give ear to
19	幣原(しではら)　喜重郎(きじゅうろう)	1872–1951, 総理大臣, 1945–1946
	提案(ていあん)	proposal, proposition
20	占領軍(せんりょうぐん)	army of occupation

〔p. 59〕

21	ホイットニー	Whitney, a U.S. General
	ケーディス	Cades, a U.S. General
22	帰(き)せられる	[passive of 帰する] be due to, be attributable to, be traceable to
23	功績(こうせき)	merit, meritorious service

〔p. 60〕

2	正直(しょうじき)	honesty, integrity
3	徹底性(てっていせい)	thoroughness, exhaustiveness
	つきつめる	inquire into, examine thoroughly
4	ナショナリズム	nationalism
5	インターナショナリズム	internationalism
7	案外(あんがい)に	unexpectedly, surprisingly
	感覚(かんかく)	feeling, sensation, senses
11	東京帝国大学(とうきょうていこくだいがく)	pre-World War II name of 東京大学
	国語学(こくごがく)	study of the mother tongue, Japanese linguistics, Japanese philology
12	ちょんまげ	topknot
13	結(ゆ)う	wear (*or* fix) one's hair in a certain style
	いたるところに	everywhere, at every turn
15	ルネッサンス	renaissance
	一息(ひといき)につっきる	go through, clear at a bound. *literally*, cut over in a breath
17	序文(じょぶん)	preface

〔p. 60〕

18	同僚(どうりょう)	associate, colleague
	おえる	finish (something)
19	～なんて	*colloq.*, ＝～など
	哲学(てつがく)	philosophy
20	講義(こうぎ)	lecture
21	ならびに	as well as, and also
22	～にいやけをおこさせる	make (a person) sick of (something)
23	スイス	Switzerland

〔p. 61〕

1	失望(しつぼう)	disappointment
2	あきらかにする	reveal, make clear
3	一代(いちだい)	a generation, one's lifetime
4	かたちで	in the form of
6	ふりかえってみる	look back
	意外(いがい)に	surprisingly
8	カゴ	palanquin
	打毬(だきゅう)	Japanese polo
9	相撲(すもう)	sumo, Japanese wrestling
10	なお	still, even
11	向(む)け	for, appropriate for
12	林屋(はやしや)・辰三郎(たつさぶろう)	1914–, 歴史学(れきしがく), 京都大学人文科学研究所教授
	梅棹(うめさお) 忠夫(ただお)	1920–, 民族学(みんぞくがく), 京都大学教授
	加藤(かとう) 秀俊(ひでとし)	1930–, 社会評論家, professor at the University of Hawaii
	編(へん)	edited by
13	こめる	concentrate on, put into

〔p. 61〕

14	愛惜(あいせき)する	be loath to part with
	～つつ	*literary,* ＝～しながら
	おもかげ	shadow, trace
16	多田(ただ)　道太郎(みちたろう)	1924–, 評論家, フランス文学
	残存(ざんそん)	survival, hangover
	転生(てんせい)	transformation
17	俳句(はいく)	haiku
	カメラ	camera
	絵巻物(えまきもの)	picture scroll
18	アルバム	album
	筆(ふで)	a writing brush
	フェルトのサイン・ペン	a felt pen
19	コミュニケーション	communication
21	つらぬく	penetrate
23	重要視(じゅうようし)する	regard as important

〔p. 62〕

2	やや	somewhat
4	空(あ)き地(ち)	vacant land, an open space
5	箱庭(はこにわ)	miniature garden (*or* landscape)
6	象徴(しょうちょう)	symbol, emblem
	宇宙(うちゅう)	universe, cosmos
7	縮尺(しゅくしゃく)する	reduce in size (*or* scale)
	～し	＝～して
	術(じゅつ)	art, skill, way
9	これ	＝集中(しゅうちゅう)
10	もともと	originally, from the first
11	バイキン	germ
	顕微鏡(けんびきょう)	microscope

〔p. 62〕

11	拡大(かくだい)する	magnify, enlarge
	模型(もけい)	model, relief
12	〜とは逆(ぎゃく)に	in contrast to 〜
	ちぢめる	reduce
15	〜ほかないだろう	＝〜ほかには方法(ほうほう)がないだろう
	藩(はん)	a district governed by a feudal lord in the Edo period, feudal domain
	関所(せきしょ)	barrier, checkpoint between *han* boundaries
16	しばりつけられる	[passive of しばりつける] be bound to, be tied to
17	生涯(しょうがい)	lifetime
18	わずかな	trifling, few, insignificant
19	幕藩(ばくはん)	feudal government and *han*
21	はばまれる	[passive of はばむ] be obstructed, be impeded

〔p. 63〕

1	依然(いぜん)として	as it was before, as 〜 as ever
	ひげがうすい	a light beard. *cf.* ひげがこい, a heavy beard
	生理的(せいりてき)な	physiological
3	はすかいに	aslant, obliquely
4	当(とう)の	the said (person or thing), in question
	つがえる	fix, pair one with another
5	礼儀(れいぎ)にかなう	be polite. 礼儀, etiquette; かなう, conform to, measure up to

〔p. 63〕

6	そぶり	behavior, attitude
7	ネクタイ	necktie
	あたり	vicinity, direction
8	心得（こころえ）	directions, hints (on)
	～むき	for～, suitable for～
9	不良少年（ふりょうしょうねん）	juvenile delinquent
	ガンをつける	*slang*, keep an eye on somebody
10	因縁（いんねん）	cause and effect. ～をつける, make up a reason to start a quarrel, invent a pretext (for quarreling)
12	的（まと）を射（い）ず	without hitting the target. *cf.* 射る, shoot
13	こころざし	intention
14	眼（め）のくばりかた	a way of keeping a lookout. *cf.* 目（め）をくばる, glance around. 気（き）をくばる, be on one's guard
15	もてなしかた	a way of treating people. *cf.* もてなし, hospitality, reception
17	観察（かんさつ）	view, survey
18	礼儀正（れいぎただ）しい	well-mannered
19	とまどう	feel lost, be disoriented, be embarrassed
20	知人（ちじん）	aquaintance
	尾行（びこう）する	follow, trail, spy
21	せっかく	with trouble, at great pains

〔p. 64〕

1	目（め）の前（まえ）で	in front of a person

〔p. 64〕

2	召使い（めしつかい）	servant
3	行儀（ぎょうぎ）	manners, deportment
9	使用人（しようにん）	employee, servant
10	指示（しじ）	directions, orders
11	なになにの	such and such
13	おろか	foolish
14	～を前提（ぜんてい）として	on the assumption that ～, assuming～
15	知力（ちりょく）	intelligence
	体力（たいりょく）	physical strength
17	体格（たいかく）	physique, build, frame
21	側面（そくめん）	aspect, the side
	かぶさる	overlap
22	無能（むのう）さ	incompetence, lack of ability
	こぼす	complain, grumble
	忠実（ちゅうじつ）	faithfulness, devotion

〔p. 65〕

2	裏切（うらぎ）る	betray, disappoint
3	兼業農家（けんぎょうのうか）	farming household that supplements its income by engaging in some additional work or sideline *cf.* 兼業, side job
4	推定（すいてい）する	assume, presume
	共同体（きょうどうたい）	cooperative system
6	余暇（よか）	leisure, spare time
	増大（ぞうだい）	increase, enlarge
7	カタログ	catalogue
8	用途（ようと）	use, service

〔p. 65〕

9	マス・コミュニケーション	mass communication
10	網(あみ)の目(め)	network
	情報(じょうほう)	information
	交換(こうかん)	exchange
11	設計図(せっけいず)	outline, plan, blueprint

13 肇めに文字あり

〔p. 66〕

1	肇(はじ)めに	in the beginning
3	単行本(たんこうぼん)	volume, book
	点数(てんすう)	number
	～並(なみ)	same as ～
5	車窓(しゃそう)	windows of vehicles
	恋人(こいびと)	lover, love
7	相対的(そうたいてき)に	relatively
8	憤慨(ふんがい)する	resent, be enraged
10	原稿(げんこう)	manuscript, writing
11	～料(りょう)	fee for ～
13	執筆生活(しっぴつせいかつ)	writer's life
14	分野(ぶんや)	field (of study, etc.)
15	金属(きんぞく)	metal
	見(み)廻(ま)わす	＝見回わす, look around
16	掲示板(けいじばん)	bulletin board
17	梁(はり)	beam
	頭(あたま)下(さ)げろ	lower your head [imperative]
	栓(せん)消(しょう)火(か)	close the hydrant [imperative]
18	いたって	exceedingly, very
	あじけない	flat, insipid

〔p. 67〕

1	一杯(いっぱい)に	all over
	ベタベタはる	paste (bills) all over. ベタベタ [onomatopoeic word used as

〔p. 67〕

		an adverb]
1	整頓（せいとん）	put in order [imperative]
	責任遂行（せきにんすいこう）	accomplish responsibility [imperative]
2	発意向上（はついこうじょう）	promote motivation [imperative]
	疲労防止週間（ひろうぼうししゅうかん）	week for preventing fatigue
3	ぐうぐう寝（ね）る	sleep soundly. ぐうぐう [onomatopoeic word used as an adverb]
	ねじ	nuts
	ゆるみ	looseness
7	ゼーロ・ディフェクツ	zero defects
	おしゃか	defective article
9	横文字（よこもじ）	characters written horizontally, European languages
	頭文字（かしらもじ）	initials
10	用語（ようご）	term, vocabulary, jargon
	頻繁（ひんぱん）に	frequently
13	例（れい）の	habitual, usual. *cf.* 例のごとく, as is usually the case with
	スローガン	slogan
14	カッとする	to be excited, angry
	事故（じこ）	accident
15	運転手（うんてんしゅ）	driver, operator
16	交通局（こうつうきょく）	traffic bureau
17	心境（しんきょう）とくると	when it comes to one's state (*or* frame) of mind

〔p. 67〕

17	それこそ	very
	悦(えつ)に入(い)る	be satisfied, be pleased (about something)
18	大(おお)いに～のために尽(つく)す	do much for, render service to
19	にっこり笑(わら)う	have a big smile, grin
	さぞ	＝大変(たいへん). さぞ～であろう，How～ (one) is!
21	壁訓名言(へきくんめいげん)	short maxim posted on a wall
23	～ぶり	manner of～

〔p. 68〕

1	機械工(きかいこう)	factory hand, machine operator, mechanic
	発動機(はつどうき)	motor, engine
	クシャクシャになっている	to be crumpled. クシャクシャ, crumpled, disheveled [onomatopoeic word used as an adjective]
2	青図(あおず)	＝青写真(あおじゃしん), blueprint
	参考(さんこう)	reference, consult
4	カン(勘)	intuition, perception, feel
	コツ(骨)	knack
5	ワーク・ブック	workbook
	細部(さいぶ)にわたる	go into detail
6	羅列(られつ)する	arrange in a row
7	虎(とら)の巻(まき)	manual, pony
	果(はた)して	[by this adverb the author must have meant ほんとうに but this is an incorrect usage of

〔p. 68〕

the adverb 果して, which means 'just as the speaker expected,' or 'is it really . . .?' in an interrogative sentence],果して注意したかという〜.*if* he really paid attention

8	日課記録帳（にっかきろくちょう）	daily records
12	無駄（むだ）	waste, useless
13	媒介（ばいかい）	medium, agent
	趣き（おもむき）	taste, purpose
14	技能者（ぎのうしゃ）	skilled worker
	見習工（みならいこう）	apprentice
15	無事に（ぶじに）	safely, without accident
	一人前の（いちにんまえの）	respectable, self-supporting
16	熟練工（じゅくれんこう）	skilled worker
17	奨励する（しょうれいする）	encourage
19	一応（いちおう）	at least, somehow
	パス	pass
20	技術養成所（ぎじゅつようせいじょ）	vocational school, trade school
22	名刺（めいし）	name card, business card
23	苗字（みょうじ）	family name
	〔p. 69〕	
2	見極める（みきわめる）	ascertain
	交際する（こうさいする）	keep company with
4	まともな	honest, upright
	確乎たる（かっこたる）	firm, determined. 〜たる＝〜とした

〔p. 69〕

5	ひそむ	lie behind, be latent
6	喜怒哀楽（きどあいらく）	joy, anger, sadness and happiness
	しかり	*literary*, ＝そうである
	訴（うった）える	have recourse to, appeal
8	曇天（どんてん）	cloudy
	やや	*adv.*, little
	幸子（さちこ）	a female given name
9	家出（いえで）	leaving home, running away from home
	実家（じっか）	one's parents' house [from the point of view of a married woman]
	無味乾燥（むみかんそう）	dry and uninteresting
11	終止符（しゅうしふ）	period, end
12	熱（ねつ）っぽい	ardent, passionate
	ティーンエージャー	teen-ager
13	紙上（しじょう）に	on paper, in black and white
	気（き）がすまない	be dissatisfied with, feel regret for. *cf.* 気がすむ, be satisfied, be gratified
15	感謝状（かんしゃじょう）	letter of thanks, appreciation
	賞状（しょうじょう）	certificate of merit, testimonial
16	せいぜい	at most
17	洗礼（せんれい）	baptism
	証明書（しょうめいしょ）	certificate
18	農協（のうきょう）の青婦委員（せいふいいん）	members of the young men and women's division of a farm-

〔p. 69〕

		er's cooperative
19	福祉（ふくし）	welfare
21	額（がく）	frame (of a picture, etc.)
22	旅館（りょかん）	Japanese-style inn
	勝手（かって）	kitchen
	傑作（けっさく）	masterpiece
23	遊興飲食税（ゆうきょういんしょくぜい）	tax for food and entertainment
	府政（ふせい）	(Kyoto) prefectural government
	念（ねん）にもえ	＝念にもえて, ardently

〔p. 70〕

1	完納（かんのう）	full payment
	心（こころ）を打（う）たれる	be moved
2	～ずにいられない	can't help but ～
	蜷川（にながわ）	元京都府知事（もときょうとふちじ）
	六選（ろくせん）する	be elected 6 times
4	後悔（こうかい）	repentance
5	始末書（しまつしょ）	written explanation
6	～と受（う）け取（と）る	understand that～
	外人登録（がいじんとうろく）	alien registration
7	おこたる	neglect, be negligent of
	警察（けいさつ）	police station
8	親切極（しんせつきわ）まる	extremely kind, most attentive
	指導（しどう）	guidance, leadership
	法務大臣（ほうむだいじん）	minister of justice
9	誤（あやま）ち	mistake, error
	自供（じきょう）する	confess
	呉々（くれぐれ）も	repeatedly

〔p. 70〕

10	大(だい)それた	＝大変(たいへん)な, outrageous, inordinate
	無法行為(むほうこうい)	unlawful behavior
	確約(かくやく)	definite promise
16	組合(くみあ)わせ	combination
	こと足(た)りる	be enough, be sufficient
18	授(さず)ける	teach, give, instruct
21	投資(とうし)する	invest
	機(き)ある毎(ごと)に	on every occasion, at every opportunity. 機＝機会(きかい)
22	発揮(はっき)する	display, demonstrate
23	意志疎通(いしそつう)	(mutual) understanding

〔p. 71〕

1	～に迷惑(めいわく)をかける	give trouble to ～
2	千差万別(せんさばんべつ)の	infinite variety of
	こみいった	complicated
3	書道(しょどう)	calligraphy, way of writing
	芸術(げいじゅつ)をなす	form an art
5	風習(ふうしゅう)	custom
6	ぶかっこうな	awkward, clumsy, unshapely
	操(あやつ)る	handle, manage
8	残念(ざんねん)に思(おも)う	regret, be disappointed, be sorry
9	習字(しゅうじ)	calligraphy, penmanship
10	目(め)にさわる	be ugly, injure one's eyes, be harmful to the eyes
	かっこのついた	shapely
	達筆(たっぴつ)の	skillful (in handwriting), good

〔p. 71〕

15	メリーランド大学（だいがく）	University of Maryland
	マックギンネス	McGuinness, psychologist
	実験（じっけん）	experiment, laboratory work
	しくみ(仕組)	plan, construction
17	ヴェトナム	Vietnam
19	猛反対（もうはんたい）	severe opposition
20	グループ	group
	かた方（ほう）	one side
	ニックソン	Nixon, Richard M.
	弁護（べんご）する	speak in favor of, justify
21	パンフレット	pamphlet
22	文章（ぶんしょう）	sentence
	テープ	tape
	ふきこむ	record

〔p. 72〕

1	録音（ろくおん）	transcription, recorded tape
2	弁護論（べんごろん）	advocacy, vindication
8	納得（なっとく）のいく	satisfactory, to a person's satisfaction
9	表意文字（ひょういもじ）	hieroglyph, ideograph
	表音文字（ひょうおんもじ）	phonetic alphabet
	達成（たっせい）	achievement, accomplishment
11	広範囲（こうはんい）	a vast range, a wide scope
12	ギリシャ	Greece
13	ロゴス	Logos, the Word
14	修正（しゅうせい）する	modify, amend

14 日本と西洋

〔p. 73〕

3	村上（むらかみ）	a person's family name
	畏怖感（いふかん）	awe, state of being awed
4	本能的に（ほんのうてき）	instinctively
	しみつく	be deeply dyed with
	典型的な（てんけいてき）	typical
6	甘やかす（あま）	indulge (children), spoil (children)
	乱暴に（らんぼう）	roughly, carelessly
	勝手気ままな（かってき）	selfish, having one's own way
7	ふるまい	behavior
8	見習う（みなら）	receive training
11	紳士（しんし）	gentleman
12	文字どおり（もじ）	literally
	大人しい（おとな）	well-behaved like an adult, gentle, quiet
13	目が光る（め・ひか）	＝見ている（み）, watch
	～かぎりにおいて	as long as ～, provided that ～
14	甘い（あま）	lenient, sweet
	なめてかかる	underrate, despise
15	一変する（いっぺん）	change completely
16	口をそろえて（くち）	unanimously, in chorus
	偽善（ぎぜん）	hypocrisy
17	たまらない	be unbearable, be more than one can stand

〔p. 73〕

17	おもちゃ	toy
	ひっぱり出(だ)す	＝引(ひ)き出す
	夢中(むちゅう)になる	be carried away, be fascinated
19	いじきたなくせがむ	ask greedily
	はては	in the end

〔p. 74〕

1	戸棚(とだな)	closet, cabinet
4	しり	one's behind, the buttocks
	とりわけ	especially
	たきぎ	firewood
5	頑丈(がんじょう)な	sturdy
	掌(てのひら)	palm
	痛(いた)み	pain, ache
	やきつく	be deeply impressed
7	街角(まちかど)	street corner
	泣(な)きわめく	cry out
	耳(みみ)たぶ	earlobe
	グイグイとひっぱる	pull with all one's strength. グイグイと [onomatopoeic word used as an adverb]
8	光景(こうけい)	scene, spectacle
	肉体的(にくたいてき)な	corporal, physical
11	恐怖心(きょうふしん)	fear
	機嫌(きげん)	mood, temper
12	すばやい	quick
	いったん	once
	組(く)みしやすい	be easy to deal with
13	本能(ほんのう)	instinct

〔p. 74〕

13	制御（せいぎょ）	control
14	結論（けつろん）	conclusion
15	評論家（ひょうろんか）	critic
20	馴（な）らす	tame
	すれちがう	pass by each other
21	吠（ほ）えかかる	bark at. ～に吠えかかる
	同士（どうし）	a fellow-, the same kind

〔p. 75〕

1	～ことにかけて	as far as ～ is concerned, in (doing something)
3	根気（こんき）	patience, tolerance
	目先（めさき）の	immediate, before one's eyes
	ほうび	reward, prize
4	しつこく	persistently, repeatedly
	条件反射（じょうけんはんしゃ）	conditioned reflex
10	それにつけても	even in this condition
	植物（しょくぶつ）	plant, vegetation
11	長（ちょう）じている	＝すぐれている, excel in, be accomplished in. ～に長じている
12	同化（どうか）する	adapt oneself to, assimilate
13	～を屈伏（くっぷく）させる	force someone to give in
14	価値感（かちかん）	sense of value
17	仮説（かせつ）	hypothesis
18	自発的（じはつてき）	spontaneous, voluntary
19	自律的（じりつてき）	autonomous, self-controlled
22	希薄（きはく）	thinness, rarity

〔p. 76〕

1	テーブルマナーズ	table manners

〔p. 76〕

2	乗物	vehicle, a (public) conveyance
3	保持する	maintain, preserve
5	反省	reconsideration, reflection
6	暴露	exposure, disclosure
	残虐	atrocity, cruelty
8	なかろう	＝ないであろう
9	戦中派	people who grew up during World War II
10	情緒的	emotional
	世代感覚	feelings of a generation
	湿度	humidity
12	モンスーン	monsoon
	地帯	zone
13	ウェット	wet
	和辻　哲郎	1889–1960, 倫理学, 文化史
14	博士	Dr., Ph.D.
	牧場	pasture, meadow
15	乾燥した	dry, parched, arid
16	財力	wealth
17	額面	face value, appearance, mere outlook
19	奥さん	wife (of another)
21	称号	title
22	ドクトル	Doktor [from German], doctor
	～はもとより～までも	＝～ばかりでなく～も

〔p. 77〕

4	ばかに	＝とくに, ridiculously, extremely

〔p. 77〕

5	遠慮(えんりょ)する	be reserved, be modest
	しりごむ	hesitate, draw back
	謙遜(けんそん)する	be humble
	美徳(びとく)	virtue, grace
6	事務官(じむかん)	administrative official, secretary
	はたから	=他の人から, by others, from the outside
7	笑(わら)われもする	=笑われさえする
	みじんもない	=全然(ぜんぜん)ない
8	ヒットラー	Hitler, Adolf
9	易々(いい)として	=とても簡単(かんたん)に, easily
	虐殺(ぎゃくさつ)	slaughter
	おもむく(赴く)	=行く
10	謎(なぞ)	puzzle, riddle
13	ナチス	the Nazis
	なんら	=ぜんぜん〜ない, in any way [with neg.]
14	〜を問(と)わない	apply equally to
15	共産主義(きょうさんしゅぎ)	communism
	脅威(きょうい)	threat, intimidation
17	極端(きょくたん)	an extreme
18	断言(だんげん)	assert positively
19	冠(かん)たる	*adj.*, being the first, best
20	プラーグ	Prague
21	首脳(しゅのう)	leaders, the brains
22	〜ではないかな	=〜ではないだろうか
23	東欧諸国(とうおうしょこく)	Eastern European nations

	〔p. 77〕	
23	肩(かた)で風(かぜ)を切(き)る	strut along, swagger about
	〔p. 78〕	
1	うなずく	nod, agree
3	正面切(しょうめんき)って	in front, in public, openly
5	～どころか	S_1～S_2 [by using どころか one negates the content of S_1 in order to emphasize the content of S_2], far from ～, instead of～
	やっつける	beat, defeat
8	ハインリッヒ・ベル	Heinrich Bell
9	ホーフフート	Hochhuth, Rolf
	反論(はんろん)	counterargument
10	課題(かだい)	theme, subject
11	テーマ	theme
14	浴(あ)びるほど	as if one were bathed in～
	かぐ	smell
	デリケート	delicate
15	傷(きず)	a wound, an injury
	～ことなく	without ～ing
	いきなり	suddenly, without notice
	たちむかう	confront
16	粗大(そだい)な	coarse, rough
17	肌(はだ)あい	disposition, nature
18	帰結(きけつ)	consequence, result
19	ゆく手(て)	the way, one's destination
	懸念(けねん)	fear, anxiety
	いだく（抱く）	＝心(こころ)の中(なか)に持(も)つ, have

〔p. 78〕

21	携帯（けいたい）する	carry with, bring
22	青春（せいしゅん）	youth
23	絶望（ぜつぼう）	despair, hopelessness
	不在（ふざい）	absence

〔p. 79〕

1	乖離（かいり）	alienation, estrangement
2	悲惨（ひさん）	misery
3	即事的訴（そくじてきうった）え	direct appeal
	抽象的（ちゅうしょうてき）	abstract
4	思念（しねん）	thought
5	たりうる	＝でありうる, possible to be
	ベルリン	Berlin
	田中（たなか）　路子（みちこ）	a person's name
7	想起（そうき）する	＝思（おも）い出（だ）す
	かつて	once (in the past)
8	遺稿（いこう）	posthumous works
9	感傷（かんしょう）	sentimentality
	反映（はんえい）	influence, reflection
12	矛盾（むじゅん）する	contradict
13	竹山（たけやま）　道雄（みちお）	1903–, ドイツ文学
14	一文（いちぶん）	an article
17	石田（いしだ）　英一郎（えいいちろう）	1903–1968, 文化人類（じんるい）学

15 結婚観の変遷(抄)

〔p. 80〕

1	変遷（へんせん）	change, transition
	抄（しょう）	excerpt
2	仲人（なこうど）	go-between, matchmaker
3	方式（ほうしき）	method, way
	うんと	*colloq.*, ＝たいへん, たくさん, very
5	一般庶民（いっぱんしょみん）	common people
	田舎（いなか）	rural district, the country
6	維新（いしん）	the (Meiji) Restoration, renovation
7	封建割拠（ほうけんかっきょ）	independent local government in the feudal era
8	出歩く（であるく）	go about, go out
9	従来（じゅうらい）の	former, up to this point. *cf.* 従来, *adv.*, hitherto
10	作用（さよう）する	effect, function
11	おのずから	naturally, by itself
	通婚圏（つうこんけん）	the range of marriage
12	配偶者（はいぐうしゃ）	spouse, mate
13	異性（いせい）	opposite sex
	目（め）が肥（こ）える	be experienced
15	みとおす	see through
	かえって	[what follows かえって is a result contrary to one's expectation] on the contrary

〔p. 80〕

15	恋愛（れんあい）	love affair
16	用意（ようい）する	arrange for, provide for
17	失敗（しっぱい）	failure, mistake
18	養成（ようせい）する	cultivate (an ability), develop (an ability)
19	若者組（わかものぐみ）	young men's association
	娘組（むすめぐみ）	young women's association
	宿（やど）	community house

〔p. 81〕

1	管理機関（かんりきかん）	managing agency
	村内婚（そんないこん）	marriage between residents of the same village
	かたまる	group together, gather
	村外婚（そんがいこん）	marriage between residents of different locales
2	阻止（そし）する	prevent, obstruct
	子女（しじょ）	children
3	～をめぐって	concerning～, on the subject of～
	仲裁（ちゅうさい）	mediation, arbitration
4	口（くち）をきく	speak or act as a go-between
	をも	*emphatic,* ＝を
	辞（じ）する	decline, excuse oneself from. ～をも辞さない, be prepared to ～
6	ご承知（しょうち）のように	＝ごぞんじのように, as you know
	いろんな	*colloq.,* ＝いろいろな
7	伸張（しんちょう）する	extend, expand

〔p. 81〕

8	即応する	conform to, agree with
9	枠	frame, framework
	一向に	not～ at all [with neg.]
10	いたずらに	in vain, for nothing
11	はばむ(阻む)	obstruct
	おれ	I [male informal speech]
12	よそ者	outsider
14	制裁する	take sanctions, punish
	酒食	saké, wine and food
15	金品	money and goods
	強要する	extort, demand persistently
	夜這い	stealing into a house to see a woman
17	すたって	=すたれて. すたれる, die out, go out of use
	潰滅	demolition, annihilation
18	日清戦争	Sino-Japanese War, 1894–1895
19	青年会	young men's association
	処女会	young women's association
23	断絶する	cut off, be severed

〔p. 82〕

2	性教育	sex education
	ときたま	sometimes
3	勇敢に	bravely, courageously
	もとめる(求める)	want, seek
	すれっからし	hussy, saucy girl
	あばずれ	vixen, shameless woman
5	保障する	guarantee

〔p. 82〕

8	すいもからいもしりつくした人（ひと）	experienced person. *literally*, person with sour and bitter experience
10	素地（そじ）ができる	have a grounding in ～, be the groundwork for～
11	閑人（ひまじん）	man of leisure
12	ひきうける	accept, undertake, take (a matter) into one's hands
13	転換期（てんかんき）	turning point, transition
14	ましな	better, preferable
16	配慮（はいりょ）	concern, solicitude
17	働（はたら）かずとも	＝働かなくても
	隠居（いんきょ）	person retired from active life
18	寄生地主（きせいじぬし）	landowner who lives off the labor of his tenants. *cf.* 寄生, parasite
19	手作地主（てさくじぬし）	landowner who cultivates his own land
20	遊蕩（ゆうとう）	dissipation, profligacy
	投機（とうき）	speculation, stockbroking
21	選挙運動（せんきょうんどう）	election campaign
	たずさわる	participate in, be a party to. ～にたずさわる
	出雲（いずも）の神様（かみさま）	Shinto gods of Izumo Shrine who were believed to insure a sound marriage. *colloq.*, a go-between

〔p. 82〕

23	福沢（ふくざわ） 諭吉（ゆきち）	1834–1901，思想家（しそうか），慶応（けいおう）大学創立（そうりつ）者（しゃ）

〔p. 83〕

2	当事者（とうじしゃ）	the party (*or* person) concerned
3	いよいよ	finally
5	〜と趣（おもむき）を異（こと）にする	be of a different nature
7	帯（おび）に短（みじか）したすきに長（なが）し	useless, good neither for one thing nor another. *literally*, too short for an *obi* (belt) and too long for a *tasuki* (sash for tying back the sleeves of a kimono)
	思案（しあん）する	think about
9	意向（いこう）	inclination, intention, idea
	異存（いぞん）	objection
11	発案者（はつあんしゃ）	proposer, person who suggests
	決議者（けつぎしゃ）	decision maker
12	候補者（こうほしゃ）	candidate
14	取（と）るに足（た）らない	be trivial, be unimportant
15	斬（き）りすてる	put a man to the sword, cut down
16	名目上（めいもくじょう）	formally, nominally
17	世（よ）の中（なか）は広（ひろ）いもので	*idiom*, the world is wider than it appears
18	銭（ぜに）	*archaic*, money
19	威光（いこう）	power, influence
	嫁入（よめいり）	marriage [for women]
	酔狂（すいきょう）で	on a whim, for fun. *literally*,

〔p. 83〕

		drunk and mad
20	路傍（ろぼう）	roadside, wayside
	小民（しょうみん）	unimportant people, little people
	手打（てう）ちにする	put to the sword
	情知（なさけし）らず	pitiless
	人非人（にんぴにん）	devil, inhuman shape
22	概（がい）していえば	generally speaking
	不平（ふへい）	complaint, dissatisfaction

〔p. 84〕

3	せっかち	haste
5	おおむね	mostly
	正論（せいろん）	just argument, fair argument
7	裏（うら）づける	back up, support
	結構（けっこう）	fairly well, tolerably
11	親身（しんみ）	a relative. 〜になって, heartily, earnestly
12	奔走（ほんそう）する	run about, be busy about
	膳立（ぜんだ）てをする	prepare. *literally*, set the table for dinner
13	有力者（ゆうりょくしゃ）	influential person
16	はで	gaiety, gaudiness
17	栄誉（えいよ）	honor, glory
	そえる	add, attach
20	座敷仲人（ざしきなこうど）	"parlor" go-between, ceremonial go-between
	盃仲人（さかずきなこうど）	"saké cup" go-between, ceremonial go-between

〔p. 84〕

20	横着(おうちゃく)な	idle, lazy
21	運動屋(うんどうや)	＝選挙(せんきょ)運動をする人
22	とびつく	jump at, snatch at
	～組(くみ)	～pair
23	手合(てあ)い	fellow, chap

〔p. 85〕

2	粗末(そまつ)	roughness, coarseness, poorness
3	目当(めあ)てに	aiming for, in hopes of
5	くっつける	join, marry (persons)
6	詐欺(さぎ)	fraud
	類(るい)する	be similar to, be like. ～に類する
7	～の代名詞(だいめいし)	synonym for～, another name for～, pronoun of～
	仲人口(なこうどぐち)	saying only nice things about persons, matchmaker's story
10	放棄(ほうき)する	abandon, resign
12	多分(たぶん)に	much, a great deal
13	考慮(こうりょ)	consideration, deliberation
14	出世(しゅっせ)	rising in the world, success in life
	野心(やしん)	ambition
16	変則的(へんそくてき)な	anomalous, unnatural
17	玉(たま)の輿(こし)	bejeweled palanquin, a woman of no birth marrying a famous or wealthy man
19	てづる(手づる)	connections
	養子縁組(ようしえんぐみ)	adoption

〔p. 86〕

1	狡猾（こうかつ）なる	＝狡猾な, cunning, sly
	策略（さくりゃく）	strategy, tactics, plan
	うまうまと	successfully, nicely
	のせる	take in
	これはまた	[また indicates surprise on the part of the speaker or writer] indeed!
2	あてられる	be ill at ease, be annoyed
4	世間（せけん）しらずの	ignorant of the world, unworldly
	坊（ぼ）っちゃん	boy
	嬢（じょう）ちゃん	girl
	立身（りっしん）	rising in society, social climbing
5	～組（ぐみ）	group, class
	奥野（おくの） 信太郎（しんたろう）	1899–1968, 随筆家, 中国（ちゅうごく）文学
	『はるかな女（おんな）たち』	book title, *Women in My Memory*
7	海軍兵曹（かいぐんへいそう）	naval warrant officer
	遺子（いし）	child of the deceased, orphan
	相州（そうしゅう）	＝相模（さがみ）, a Tokugawa era province
	神奈川県（かながわけん）	Kanagawa prefecture
	小坪（こつぼ）の産（さん）	native of Kotsubo [place-name]
8	逗子（ずし）	place-name
9	養神亭（ようしんてい）	a name of a Japanese-style restaurant
	一高（いっこう）	First High School [proper name]

〔p. 86〕

9	優等（ゆうとう）	honor graduate
	成績（せいせき）	marks, score, rating
	岩崎（いわさき）	1834–1885, 明治時代（めいじじだい）の実業家
10	要領（ようりょう）のいい	clever, smart
11	ドンファン	Don Juan
	平生（へいぜい）	*adv.*, everyday, usually
	口（くち）ぐせ	one's favorite phrase, a way of saying
	もち崩（くず）す	ruin oneself
12	奴（やつ）	fellow, chap
	ふける	be addicted to, indulge in. 〜にふける
	あやまりなく	without a slip, without error
13	街道（かいどう）	highway, thoroughfare
	驀進（ばくしん）する	dash forward, dart
	頼（たの）もしい	promising, person with a great future, reliable
	地（じ）でゆく	play a role in real life, live out a story, put an idea into action
14	かかわりあう	be involved with, have a relationship with
	目（め）もくれず	ignore, pay no attention to
15	郡長（ぐんちょう）	governor of a province
	ふり出（だ）し	beginning, start
	書記官（しょきかん）	secretary
16	総裁（そうさい）	prime minister
	息（いき）もつかせず	giving a person not a moment's

〔p. 86〕

	respite, without taking breath
18 がめつい奴(やつ)	selfish and aggressive fellow
19 閨閥(けいばつ)	nepotism
20 権勢家(けんせいか)	a man of influence
合作(がっさく)	collaboration
23 神島(かみしま) 二郎(じろう)	1918–, 日本政治思想史, 立教(りっきょう)大学法学部教授

16　明治維新と壬申戸籍

〔p. 87〕

1	壬申（じんしん）	1872 [according to the pre-Meiji year-counting system]
	戸籍（こせき）	census register, family register
2	下級武士（かきゅうぶし）	low-ranking samurai
	～なる	*literary*, = ～である
3	スポンサー	sponsor
4	ジャンル	genre
5	で	=それで
6	2本差した（にほんさした）	carrying two swords (i.e., samurai)
7	旧大名連（きゅうだいみょうれん）	feudal lords of old
8	虫けら扱いにする（むしけらあつかいにする）	treat people badly like worms
10	藩制（はんせい）	feudal clan system
	ほどほどの	in moderation, within measure
	自由勝手（じゆうがって）	unfettered state, freedom
11	儒教的道徳（じゅきょうてきどうとく）	Confucian morality
12	～簿（ぼ）	(record) book of～
	序列（じょれつ）	order, rank
	変更（へんこう）	change, modification
13	宗門帳（しゅうもんちょう）	census register up to 1871
	成員（せいいん）	member
	記載（きさい）	recording, entry, mention
	世帯主（せたいぬし）	head of a household
14	弟妹（ていまい）	younger brothers and sisters

〔p. 87〕

14	後家(ごけ)	widow
15	～本位(ほんい)の	on the basis of～. *cf.* 営利(えいり)本位の学校, a school run for profit, 児童(じどう)本位の教育, child-centered education

〔p. 88〕

2	改(あらた)まる	undergo a change, be modified
	家長(かちょう)	head of a family
3	戸主(こしゅ)	head of a household
8	滋賀県(しがけん)	Shiga prefecture
	伊香郡高時村古橋(いかぐんたかときむらふるはし)	place-name
	惣三郎(そうざぶろう)	a male given name
	女房(にょうぼう)	wife [humble form]
9	勘六(かんろく)	a male given name
	妹(いもうと)	younger sister
10	林左衛門(りんざえもん)	a male given name
	倅(せがれ)	son [humble form]
11	平之助(へいのすけ)	a male given name
12	大阪府(おおさかふ)	Osaka prefecture
	豊能郡西能勢村神山(とよのぐんにしのせむらかみやま)	place-name
	藤兵衛(とうべえ)	a male given name
	藤五郎(とうごろう)	a male given name
13	角之助(かくのすけ)	a male given name
	角太郎(かくたろう)	a male given name
	孫(まご)	grandchild
14	半助(はんすけ)	a male given name
	重三郎(じゅうざぶろう)	a male given name
15	母子家族(ぼしかぞく)	fatherless family

〔p. 88〕

15	たとい	＝たとえ, even though
16	目(め)がね	judgment, insight, glasses
	～次第(しだい)だ	depend on～, be conditional on～, resting with～
17	よし	*literary*, ＝たとえ
	たった	only, just
19	姉(あね)	elder sister
22	三島郡(みしまぐん)	place-name
	現(げん)	present, existing
	高槻市(たかつきし)	place-name, a city in Osaka prefecture
	唐崎(からさき)	place-name
	割合(わりあい)	percentage; ratio, rate

〔p. 89〕

3	わずか16年(じゅうろくねん)で	in 16 short years, in just 16 years
	減少(げんしょう)する	decrease, decline
4	相続(そうぞく)	inheritance, succession
	元来(がんらい)の	proper, original
	長子相続(ちょうしそうぞく)	primogeniture
5	～など	such things as～
	兄弟相続(きょうだいそうぞく)	consanguineal inheritance
	ザラにある	*colloq.*, be quite common
6	～連(れん)	clique, company
	伝(つた)える	bequeath, transmit, report
8	末子(まっし)	youngest child in a family
10	～なり	＝ ～たり
	開墾(かいこん)する	reclaim land, bring (waste

〔p. 89〕

		land) under cultivation
11	養子(ようし)	adopted legal heir, adopted child
	次子(じし)	second eldest child, next child
13	老衰(ろうすい)する	grow old and weak, become infirm with age
	充分(じゅうぶん)な	sufficient, enough
14	と	＝そうすると
	つぐ(継ぐ)	inherit, accede to
	居(い)すわる	remain in the same position, settle down
17	食(く)うや食(く)わずの	with a marginal existence
	5反百姓(ごたんびゃくしょう)	five-*tan* peasant, poor peasant. 1 反＝0.245 acres
	同居(どうきょ)する	reside with, live together
18	養(やしな)う	feed
19	分(ぶん)	share, portion
	収入(しゅうにゅう)	income, earnings
20	絶対量(ぜったいりょう)	absolute quantity, sum
21	あるわけでなし	＝あるわけではない [なし is a sentence-final form of the classical negative of the verb ある, 'be,' 'exist']
23	旧家(きゅうか)	an old family, established family
	風習(ふうしゅう)	custom
	師範(しはん)	teachers' course, normal school
	教員(きょういん)	teacher

〔p. 90〕

1	転任(てんにん)する	transfer
	定年(ていねん)	retirement age
	帰郷(ききょう)する	return to one's native place, go home
2	かしづく	wait upon, attend on. 〜にかしづく
	耕作(こうさく)する	cultivate
	末(すえ)っ子(こ)	*colloq.*, youngest child in a family
3	悶着(もんちゃく)	trouble, dispute
4	濫用(らんよう)	abuse, misuse, unlawful use
5	情(つれ)ない	pitiless, hard
6	部落(ぶらく)	village, settlement
	〜をば	[ば is a particle of emphasis that is seldom used in contemporary Japanese except in public speech or in formal writing. *cf.* contrastive は]
7	御法(ごほう)	law
	くぐる	evade, dodge, get around
	細工(さいく)しもつ	use an artifice, use tactics
8	野州郡(やすぐん)	place-name
	湖東(ことう)	region east of Lake Biwa, Shiga prefecture
11	貧農(ひんのう)	poor farmer
	山形県(やまがたけん)	Yamagata prefecture
12	無着(むちゃく)　成恭(せいきょう)	a person's name
	山(やま)びこ学校(がっこう)	book title, *School of Echoes* (a

〔p. 90〕

		collection of pupils' compositions edited by Seikyō Muchaku)
13	武家屋敷（ぶけやしき）	samurai residence
	間取り（まどり）	layout of a house, room arrangement
14	上方（かみがた）	the Kyoto–Osaka area
	田の字型（たのじがた）	shape of the character '田'
15	柱（はしら）	pillar, column
	真四角（ましかく）	square
16	玄関（げんかん）	vestibule, entry room
17	フスマ	paper-covered sliding door
18	一重（ひとえ）	one layer. *cf.* フスマ一重をへだてて, with a sliding door between
	隣室（りんしつ）	adjoining room
	成人夫婦（せいじんふうふ）	grown-up couple
	閨（ねや）	bedroom
	むつごと	sweet words, lovers' talk
19	春事（しゅんじ）	lovemaking
	機密（きみつ）	secret, inside information
	〜あったものではない	〜be out of the question
	姑（しゅうとめ）	mother-in-law
	ノイローゼになる	become neurotic. ノイローゼ, [from German, 'Neurose']
21	妻問い婚（つまどいこん）	a marriage system in which a husband only visits his wife at her residence

〔p. 90〕

21	一部（いちぶ）	＝一部の
	隠居別家（いんきょべつけ）	separate household for the retired

〔p. 91〕

1	兵庫県（ひょうごけん）	Hyōgo prefecture
	氷上郡氷上町（ひかみぐんひかみちょう）	place-name
	さる	＝ある, certain
2	廊下（ろうか）	corridor
3	帖（じょう）	＝畳（じょう）, counter for 'tatami mats' [used to describe the area of Japanese rooms]
4	地獄（じごく）	hell
5	息子夫婦（むすこふうふ）	son and his wife
6	寝間（ねま）	bedroom
	隔離（かくり）する	separate, segregate
7	親心（おやごころ）	consideration, parental affection
	～するにこしたことはない	nothing can be better than ～ing
図1	押入（おしいれ）	closet
	土間（どま）	earthen floor, an unfloored part of the house
	便所（べんじょ）	toilet
	牛小屋（うしごや）	barn
9	むごい	cruel
10	～ども	＝ ～たち
11	300年（さんびゃくねん）もつ	hold (*or* continue) for 300 years
12	崩壊（ほうかい）する	decay

〔p. 91〕

14	大身（たいしん）	man of rank, man of property
	用（よう）がない	have nothing to do with～
15	殿様（とのさま）	lord
	家老（かろう）	chief retainer, daimyo's minister
	ポツポツ	here and there, scattered [onomatopoeic word used as an adverb]
16	微禄（びろく）	small stipend, pittance

〔p. 92〕

図2	隣家（りんか）	neighboring house
	納戸（なんど）	back room, closet
	増築部（ぞうちくぶ）	an addition, added room
	卍（まんじ）	symbol for 仏壇（ぶつだん）, the household Buddhist shrine
	みそ部屋（べや）	storage room for *miso* (bean paste)
	浴室（よくしつ）	a bath, bathroom
	岡山県（おかやまけん）	Okayama prefecture
	都窪郡（つくぼぐん）	place-name
	3軒長屋（さんげんながや）	row of three similar dwellings
	奈良県（ならけん）	Nara prefecture
	添上郡小泉町（そえかみぐんこいずみちょう）	place-name
	漢学指南（かんがくしなん）	instructor in Chinese classics
	石（こく）	unit of rice by which samurai stipends were computed. 1 石 = about 5 bushels
	2軒長屋（にけんながや）	two-family house, duplex

	〔p. 92〕	
図2	物見窓（ものみまど）	window
	待合室（まちあいしつ）	waiting room
	若夫婦（わかふうふ）	young married couple
	診察間（しんさつま）	doctor's office
	座敷（ざしき）	drawing room
	多紀郡篠山町（たきぐんしのやまちょう）	place-name
	徒士（かち）	foot soldier, bannerman
	島根県（しまねけん）	Shimane prefecture
	鹿足郡津和野町（かのあしぐんつわのちょう）	place-name
	森　鷗外（もり　おうがい）	1862–1922, 医師（いし）, 小説家（しょうせつか）
	生家（せいか）	house where a person was born
	藩医（はんい）	a doctor serving a feudal clan
	〔p. 93〕	
図2	(井)	symbol for 井戸（いど）, well
	ながし	sink
	鳥取県（とっとりけん）	Tottori prefecture
	倉吉市（くらよしし）	place-name
	足軽（あしがる）	lowest ranking samurai, foot soldier
	福井県（ふくいけん）	Fukui prefecture
	大野市（おおのし）	place-name
1	改造（かいぞう）する	remodel, renovate
	やっとこさと	*colloq.*, at last, with much effort
3	予想（よそう）	expectation, presumption
4	軽輩（けいはい）	insignificant person, petty official
	食（く）い違（ちが）い型（がた）	crisscross pattern, interlocking pattern

〔p. 93〕

5	隔絶(かくぜつ)する	blockade, be isolated from
6	一対(いっつい)	a pair (of rooms)
	重(かさ)ねて言(い)うが	let me mention once again that
8	形態(けいたい)	form, shape
11	否(いな)	*literary*, ＝いや, no, or rather
	武家法(ぶけほう)	laws for samurai
12	明治憲法(めいじけんぽう)	the Meiji Constitution, 1889
	殺生(せっしょう)な	cruel
14	姉家督制(しかとくせい)	inheritance system in which the oldest daughter succeeds to the estate

〔p. 94〕

1	耕作面積(こうさくめんせき)	farming area, area under cultivation
2	農繁期(のうはんき)	(busy) farming season
	ピーク	peak
	人手(ひとで)	worker, a hand
	要(い)る	need
	日雇(ひやと)い	day laborer
	まかなう	supply, provide
3	～といったわけから	probably because of that～
4	聟(むこ)	son-in-law
	つがす	＝つがせる, let N succeed, let N inherit. *cf.* つぐ, succeed, inherit
5	母系婚(ぼけいこん)	marriage through the maternal line
	堅(かた)く	firmly

〔p. 94〕

6	やりくりする	manage (with what one has), shift with
8	こわす	destroy, break down
	おしい	regrettable, disappointing
10	窮屈(きゅうくつ)な	narrow, stiff
	昔(むかし)っから	*colloq.*, ＝昔から
11	蒲生郡(がもうぐん)T村(むら)D部落(ぶらく)	place-name
12	村方文書(むらかたぶんしょ)	village records (*or* archives)
13	古老(ころう)	old man
15	その折(おり)	＝その時(とき)
	発言力(はつげんりょく)	right to speak, (right to) a voice
16	氏神(うじがみ)	tutelary deity (of a place), *genius loci*
	神事(じんじ)	divine service, worship
	古来(こらい)	＝昔から
	参画(さんかく)する	participate in planning
17	奉仕(ほうし)する	attend, serve
	天神宮(てんじんぐう)	a shrine dedicated to Sugawara no Michizane (845–903), Minister of the Right in the Heian court
	祭礼帳(さいれいちょう)	book of festival rites
	くる	＝めくる, turn over (pages)
18	餅宿(もちやど)	host of a festival, festival sponsor
20	だいたい	＝そもそも, originally, primarily
	総元締(そうもとじめ)	headquarters, controller (of the

〔p. 94〕

		whole)
21	伊勢神宮(いせじんぐう)	Ise Shrine
	天照大神(あまてらすおおみかみ)	Goddess Amaterasu Ōmikami
	祀る(まつる)	deify
	祭祀(さいし)	Shinto ceremony
22	倭姫命(やまとひめのみこと)	legendary patroness of Ise Shrine, daughter of Suinin Tennō, eleventh emperor of Japan
	代々(だいだい)	for generations, hereditary
	斎宮(さいぐう)	(unmarried) imperial princesses serving at Ise Shrine

〔p. 95〕

1	祭祀権(さいしけん)	power to hold a religious service
2	取り上げる(とりあげる)	take away, revoke
	かわっちゃった	*very colloq.*, ＝かわってしまった
3	巻き返す(まきかえす)	repeat
6	在来法(ざいらいほう)	conventional regulation, traditional law
7	似かよう(にかよう)	resemble closely
9	のみこむ	swallow, understand
12	まね	＝こと, behavior
14	さき様(さきさま)	＝相手(あいて)
	要望(ようぼう)	request
15	本人同志(ほんにんどうし)	persons (in question) themselves
16	第3者(だいさんしゃ)	third person
	介入させる(かいにゅうさせる)	let some one intervene

〔p. 95〕

17	河内(かわち)の小作百姓(こさくびゃくしょう)	tenant farmer from Kawachi [place-name]
	～の出(で)	＝～の出身(しゅつしん), come from, hail from
	江州(ごうしゅう)	＝近江(おうみ), pre-Meiji name of Shiga prefecture
19	逸聞(いつぶん)	story which is not widely known
20	懐旧(かいきゅう)	yearning for the old days
	年代記(ねんだいき)	chronicle
21	食物史(しょくもつし)	history of food
	服飾史(ふくしょくし)	history of clothing
	～こそ	with ～ing, only when
22	憶い出(おもいで)	remembrances
	話の泉(はなしのいずみ)	a popular postwar radio quiz program, "Information Please"
23	在り方(ありかた)	the way that something should be
	サゼスト	suggest

〔p. 96〕

1	なるを	*literary*, ＝～であることを
2	ゆめゆめ	never [with neg.]
4	篠田(しのだ)　統(おさむ)	1899–, 生化学(せいか), 食品化学(しょくひん), 四条(しじょう)たわて学園女子短期大学教授
	長崎(ながさき)　多美子(たみこ)	1912–, 栄養学(えいよう), 家政学(かせい), 手塚山学院講師(てづかやま)

17 家元制度

〔p. 97〕

1	家元（いえもと）	main branch of a family (in the arts)
3	おどり	Japanese style of dancing
	狂言（きょうげん）	traditional comic play
	長唄（ながうた）	traditional ballad singing, a long epic song
	常磐津（ときわず）	Tokiwazu ballad. *cf.* Jōruri
4	清元（きよもと）	Kiyomoto ballad-drama
	師匠（ししょう）	master, teacher
	連鎖（れんさ）	link, chain
5	派閥（はばつ）	clique, faction
6	擬制（ぎせい）せられる	＝擬制される, be fictitious
7	俳優（はいゆう）	actor, player
8	尾上家（おのえけ）	the Onoes, one of the families engaged in the performance of Kabuki
	市川家（いちかわけ）	the Ichikawas, one of the families engaged in the performance of Kabuki
	該当（がいとう）する	correspond to
9	宗家（そうけ）	head family
	家号（やごう）	(hereditary) stage name
	名乗（なの）る	call oneself, identify oneself as
10	周知（しゅうち）の	known to all, universally known

	〔p. 97〕	
12	領域（りょういき）	domain, sphere, territory
13	枢軸（すうじゅく）	pivot, axle, cardinal point
	支柱（しちゅう）	support, prop
14	障害（しょうがい）	obstacle, impediment
15	死活（しかつ）	life and death
17	あんま	massage
	はり	acupuncture
	〔p. 98〕	
3	本稿（ほんこう）	this article, this book
	便宜上（べんぎじょう）	as a matter of convenience
	舞踊（ぶよう）	dance
5	大観（たいかん）する	take a general view of
7	総覧（そうらん）	conspectus, synopsis
8	名取（なと）り	holder of an art name
	門弟（もんてい）	follower, disciple
	花柳流（はなやぎりゅう）	Hanayagi school
9	藤間（ふじま）	Fujima (school)
	若柳（わかやぎ）	Wakayagi (school)
10	吾妻（あずま）	Azuma (school)
	岩井（いわい）	Iwai (school)
11	小規模（しょうきぼ）の	small-scale
12	曙（あけぼの）	Akebono (school)
	神崎（かんざき）	Kanzaki (school)
	小寺（こでら）	Kodera (school)
	坂本（さかもと）	Sakamoto (school)
	新家元（しんいえもと）	new *iemoto*
13	能楽界（のうがくかい）	the world of Noh
	ギルド	guild

	〔p. 98〕	
13	群雄割拠(ぐんゆうかつきょ)	rivalry of local leaders
15	有為転変(ういてんぺん)	ups and downs of human life
17	要点(ようてん)は～にある	the essential point is that～
20	統率(とうそつ)する	lead, command
	〔p. 99〕	
5	広汎(こうはん)な	extensive, comprehensive
6	～のごとくである	＝ ～のとおりである
14	しぐさ	gestures, action
	まねる	imitate
16	厳禁(げんきん)する	forbid firmly
18	バレー	ballet
	ピアノ	piano
20	主眼(しゅがん)をおく	be aimed at～, put emphasis on～. ～に主眼をおく
22	風(ふう)	style, atmosphere
23	限局(げんきょく)される	be limited
	模範(もはん)	model
	〔p. 100〕	
2	腹芸(はらげい)	scheming behind the scene
	さとる	perceive, comprehend
3	ほんの	just
	要諦(ようてい)	secret (of success), cardinal point
6	使役(しえき)する	set to work, employ, use
	～つつ	＝ ～ながら
7	内弟子(うちでし)	private pupil
8	徒弟(とてい)	apprentice
10	秘伝(ひでん)	secret formula

〔p. 100〕

10	口伝（くでん）	secret (transmitted orally)
	公開（こうかい）する	open to the public
12	奥伝（おくでん）	secret tradition, secret
	奥許（おくゆるし）	secret precept, secret
	些細（ささい）な	trivial, small, petty
13	断片（だんぺん）	fragment, piece, odds and ends
17	成立過程（せいりつかてい）	process of formation
19	七（なな）つになる子（こ）	the Japanese dance "Child of Seven"
20	関の小萬（せきのこまん）	the Japanese dance "Seki no Koman" (a story about a girl Koman who lived at a checkpoint on the Tōkaidō in the Edo period)
23	三味線（しゃみせん）	three-stringed musical instrument
	琴（こと）	thirteen-stringed musical instrument
24	大工・左官（だいく・さかん）	carpenter and plasterer
25	仕込（しこ）む	train, bring up

〔p. 101〕

2	技術習熟（ぎじゅつしゅうじゅく）	mastery of a technique or skill
4	芸名（げいめい）	stage name
8	当該（とうがい）の	in question, concerned
	承認（しょうにん）	approval
11	統率者（とうそつしゃ）	leader
12	実名（じつめい）	＝本名（ほんみょう）, real name
	～たる	*literary*, ＝～である

〔p. 101〕

14	寿美(すみ)	a given stage name
16	慣行(かんこう)	tradition, (habitual) practice
	血統(けつとう)	lineage, descent
19	寿輔(じゆすけ)	a given stage name
20	直弟子(じきでし)	one's immediate pupil
	禄美(ろくみ)	a given stage name
	禄寿(ろくじゆ)	a given stage name

〔p. 102〕

5	列席者(れつせきしや)	attendants, those present
	二分家(にぶんけ)	first branch family
6	古参者(こさんしや)	senior, old-timer
	取立師匠(とりたてししよう)	patron and teacher
8	流紋(りゆうもん)	crest of the school
	盃(さかずき)	saké cup
9	扇子(せんす)	fan
10	木札(きふだ)	wooden nameplate
11	所属(しよぞく)	one's position
	資格(しかく)	qualification, capability
17	あたかも～のごとし	＝まるで ～ のようだ, just as～
23	違反(いはん)	violation

〔p. 103〕

1	破門(はもん)	excommunication
	同門者(どうもんしや)	fellow students
2	恩恵(おんけい)	benefit, favor
5	はなはだしき	*literary*, ＝はなはだしい
	振(ふ)り付(つ)け	choreography, dance composition
	～がごとき	*literary*, ＝～ようなこと

〔p. 103〕

8	自発的返上（じはつてきへんじょう）	voluntary resignation
13	ピラミッド	pyramid
14	徒弟身分（とていみぶん）	status of apprentice
	名取り格（なとりかく）	rank of teacher
15	昇格する（しょうかく）	rise in status
18	巨大な（きょだい）	huge, enormous
	要因（よういん）	main cause, primary factor

〔p. 104〕

1	たとえる	compare to, liken to
	インド	India
	カスト	caste
2	幾層か（いくそう）	some layers
	横断的（おうだんてき）	crossing, intersecting
3	カトリック	Catholic
5	いただく（頂く）	be crowned
6	固有の（こゆう）	characteristic of, inherent in
8	孤立する（こりつ）	be isolated
9	至る（いた）	reach, arrive, get to. ～に至る
11	経過（けいか）	process, course
13	才能（さいのう）	talent, ability
	名声（めいせい）	fame, reputation
17	かようにして	*literary*, ＝このようにして
18	系列（けいれつ）	line, succession
19	曾孫（ひまご）	great-grandchild

〔p. 105〕

3	従属（じゅうぞく）	dependency
	吸収する（きゅうしゅう）	absorb, assimilate
5	家内奉公人（かないほうこうにん）	servant

〔p. 105〕

8	系譜（けいふ）	genealogy, family tree
9	さかのぼる	go back to
11	超凡人（ちょうぼんじん）	a most remarkable man. 超- [prefix] super-, ultra-
	カリスマ	charisma
12	パーソナリティ	personality
14	世襲（せしゅう）	transmission by heredity. *cf.* 世襲の, hereditary
16	非日常的（ひにちじょうてき）な	unusual
	資質（ししつ）	nature
19	手本（てほん）	model, paragon
22	厳格（げんかく）に	strictly
25	氏族（しぞく）	clan, extended family
	表象（ひょうしょう）	idea, representation

〔p. 106〕

2	密接（みっせつ）に	intimately, closely
4	秘曲（ひきょく）	esoteric music
8	利害関係（りがいかんけい）	relations affecting one's own interests
9	～ことにより	=～ことによって
11	根拠（こんきょ）	basis, ground
13	借用（しゃくよう）する	borrow
14	距離（きょり）	distance, range, interval, gap
19	とりまく	surround
22	地盤（じばん）	base, sphere of influence
	縄（なわ）ばり	sphere of influence
23	相互扶助（そうごふじょ）	mutual assistance

〔p. 107〕

2	色彩（しきさい）	coloring, tint
4	—圏（けん）	[suffix] sphere, range
8	言（い）うをまたない	needless to say that〜
9	諒解（りょうかい）する	understand
	インヒビション	inhibition
11	委譲（いじょう）する	transfer
15	調整（ちょうせい）する	regulate, govern
17	バレリーナ	ballerina
18	ほどなく	＝まもなく, soon, before long
20	類型（るいけい）	type, cultural stereotype
21	何（なん）らあやしむに足（た）りない	not surprising (*or* unexpected)
22	当然視（とうぜんし）する	take for granted
	背徳行為（はいとくこうい）	immoral act

〔p. 108〕

1	さばきかねる	*literary*, be unable to handle (*or* deal with). *cf.* さばく, to settle a matter. 〜かねる, be difficult (to do), be unable (to do)
2	懇願（こんがん）する	entreat, beg earnestly
3	預（あず）ける	entrust with, give
7	和（わ）	peace, harmony
8	憚（はばか）る	be afraid of, hesitate
	冷却期間（れいきゃくきかん）	cooling-off period
9	措置（そち）	step, move, measure
12	存在理由（そんざいりゆう）	raison d'être
	例証（れいしょう）する	illustrate, exemplify
13	ほしいままに	arbitrarily, as one pleases
16	川島（かわしま）　武宜（たけよし）	1909–, 法社会学（ほうしゃかいがく）, 東京大学名誉（めいよ）教授

18　これからの日本は農業なんか止めて外国から安い食料を買えばよいというが

〔p. 109〕

4	そのへんからうかがいたい	[そのへん literally means 'around there,' an expression often used to soften directness] let me first ask you ～
5	大(おお)ざっぱに	roughly, loosely
7	反当収量(たんあたりしゅうりょう)	crop per *tan*. *cf.* 一人当(ひとりあた)り, per person
	主産地(しゅさんち)	major production areas
9	体質(たいしつ)	constitution, habit, predisposition
10	安全弁(あんぜんべん)	safety valve
13	失業者(しつぎょうしゃ)	unemployed man
15	～しておった	＝ ～していた
17	五割(ごわり)	50 percent
	小作料(こさくりょう)	tenant's rent (for using farmland)
18	所有権(しょゆうけん)	ownership
	不可侵(ふかしん)	inviolability

〔p. 110〕

4	勤労(きんろう)	labor, work
	星(ほし)をいただく	*literally*, have stars above one's head.　星をいただいて起(お)きる get up while stars are still out
6	農本主義(のうほんしゅぎ)	"agriculture first" principle

〔p. 110〕

7	農政(のうせい)	＝農業政策(のうぎようせいさく), agricultural policy
	一貫(いっかん)して	consistently, coherently
9	依(よ)らしむべし	*literary*, ＝従(した)がわせるべきだ, should be made dependent
	知(し)らしむべからず	*literary*, ＝知らせるべきでない, should be left ignorant
12	動揺(どうよう)する	suffer turmoil, be agitated, be disturbed
13	救貧(きゅうひん)	relief of the poor
	小作農民(こさくのうみん)	tenant farmers
14	補助金(ほじょきん)	subsidy, supplement, grant
16	食(く)うに困(こま)る	be difficult to make a living
	つのる	grow in intensity, become aggravated
17	爆発(ばくはつ)する	explode, erupt
18	程(ほど)よい	moderate, favorable, good
	テコ入(い)れ〔を〕する	prop up, promote. *cf.* テコ(挺子), lever
19	豊(ゆた)かな	rich
22	天井(てんじょう)	ceiling, top, peak

〔p. 111〕

1	下(した)へ流(なが)す	spread to the lower strata of society
4	争議(そうぎ)	dispute, conflict
7	農林省(のうりんしょう)	Ministry of Agriculture and Forestry
8	〜な	[sentence-final particle な indicates a fairly old male

〔p. 111〕

		speaker's wish to persuade the listener]
9	ヒューマニスティック	humanistic
10	壁(かべ)	deadlock, barrier. *cf.* 壁につきあたる, reach a deadlock
11	1930年代(ねんだい)	the 1930s
12	恐慌(きょうこう)	panic
14	弘前(ひろさき)	place-name
	連隊(れんたい)	regiment
	徴兵検査(ちょうへいけんさ)	physical examination for conscription
15	甲種(こうしゅ)	grade A. *cf.* 乙(おつ)種, grade B; 丙(へい)種, grade C
17	青年将校(せいねんしょうこう)	young officer
18	兵隊(へいたい)	soldier
21	財閥(ざいばつ)	financial clique
	ドル買(が)い	speculation in the yen by buying dollars, illegal dollar purchase
22	犠牲(ぎせい)	sacrifice
23	危(あや)うくする	endanger. *cf.* 危うい, dangerous
	短絡(たんらく)	short circuit

〔p. 112〕

1	五(ご)・一五事件(いちごじけん)	May 15th Incident, 1932
2	二(に)・二六事件(にろくじけん)	February 26th Incident, 1936
3	もっていく	＝しむける, handle (a person), treat (a person)
	満州事変(まんしゅうじへん)	Manchurian Incident, 1931

〔p. 112〕

3	日中戦争（にっちゅうせんそう）	Sino-Japanese War, 1937–1945
7	急傾斜（きゅうけいしゃ）に	rapidly. *literally*, on a steep slope
	太平洋戦争（たいへいようせんそう）	the Pacific War, 1941–1945
	ぶっ通（とお）しに	ceaselessly, continuously
10	～から～にかけて	from～ to～
13	よけて通（とお）る	avoid, dodge
16	招（よ）ぶ	call, invite
	周恩来（しゅうおんらい）	Chou En-lai
17	～あたり	＝ ～など
	軍国主義（ぐんこくしゅぎ）	militarism
18	占（うらな）う	forecast, tell fortunes
19	大（おお）きな比重（ひじゅう）を占（し）める	be of considerable importance, be preponderant
21	～は別（べつ）として	apart from～

〔p. 113〕

9	進駐（しんちゅう）する	stay, be stationed
	～なり	[something takes place and the situation changes] at the moment when
	手（て）をつける	attempt, put oneself to (a task)
13	流血事件（りゅうけつじけん）	bloodshed
15	執念（しゅうねん）	attachment, vindictive feelings
20	作（つく）らせなきゃ	*colloq.*, ＝作らせなければ
	小作（こさく）	peasant, tenant farmer
21	自作（じさく）	landed farmer, yeoman
22	差（さ）をつける	discriminate
23	狙（ねら）い	aim, purpose

〔p. 114〕

1	意欲(いよく)	will, volition
3	差額(さがく)	difference, balance, margin
6	極端(きょくたん)にいえば	if I may exaggerate
11	食糧(しょくりょう)	foodstuff, provisions
13	反応(はんのう)	reaction, response
14	やむを得(え)ない	inevitable, unavoidable
15	安泰(あんたい)	safety, security
16	敗戦(はいせん)	defeat
18	それなりに	in its own way
	下地(したじ)	groundwork, foundation
20	怨念(おんねん)	grudge, malice, hatred

〔p. 115〕

2	ウラハラ	the contrary, the opposite
9	零細(れいさい)	small, petty, poor, fragmental
11	いかんともしがたい	*literary*, ＝どうにもできない, one can't do anything about it
13	惨事(さんじ)	disaster, tragedy
16	上(あ)げなきゃ	*very colloq.*, ＝上げなくては(いけない)
18	強制供出(きょうせいきょうしゅつ)	compulsory delivery
19	召(め)し上(あ)げる	seize by authority
	飢餓(きが)	hunger, starvation
23	猛烈(もうれつ)に	terribly, violently, fiercely

〔p. 116〕

3	段(だん)ちがいに	by far
	しちゃった	*colloq.*, ＝してしまった
4	肥料(ひりょう)	fertilizer
5	農薬(のうやく)	chemicals used for agriculture

〔p. 116〕

5	たたきこむ	throw into, hammer into
	投資（とうし）	investment
6	つり合（あ）わせる	balance, match
7	ぶちこむ	dump into, put in
8	ソロバン	abacus, an account. *cf.* ～が合（あ）う, be profitable
14	量産（りょうさん）	mass production
	省力化（しょうりょくか）	reduction in man power
	利潤（りじゅん）	profit margin
16	コスト	cost
18	めいめい	each (one)
20	分割統治政策（ぶんかつとうちせいさく）	"divide and rule" policy

〔p. 117〕

1	嫉視反目（しっしはんもく）	jealousy and hostility
	競合（きょうごう）	concurrence, conflict
3	知（し）ったこっちゃねえ	*colloq.*, ＝知ったことではない, it's none of my business
	農協（のうきょう）	＝農業協同組合（のうぎょうきょうどうくみあい）, a farmers' co-operative
4	くれりゃ	*colloq.*, ＝くれれば
	マージン	margin
8	ヘクタール	hectare
	～あたり	for～, per～
	投下馬力数（とうかばりきすう）	amount of horsepower employed
16	共同作業（きょうどうさぎょう）	group work
20	ずうっと	*colloq.*, ＝ずっと

〔p. 118〕

1	消費者(しょうひしゃ)	consumer
4	上(あ)げん	*colloq.*, ＝上げない [ん is a dialectal form of ない]
7	遮断(しゃだん)する	cut off, break, intercept
	問屋(とんや)	wholesale dealer
15	歪(ゆが)み	distortion, strain
22	おって	＝いて

〔p. 119〕

2	宿命(しゅくめい)	fate, destiny
3	きっかけ	chance, opportunity, beginning
5	母(かあ)ちゃん農業(のうぎょう)	women in the family take over farming duties while the men take part-time jobs
10	従事(じゅうじ)する	practice, engage in. 〜に従事する
14	出稼(でかせ)ぎ	work away from home
	下請(したう)け工業(こうぎょう)	subcontract system, small-scale enterprise engaged in subcontracted work
15	サービス業(ぎょう)	service industry
18	リクツ(理屈)	reason, logic
20	目下(もっか)	currently, at present
	じいちゃん	grandfather

〔p. 120〕

3	効率(こうりつ)	efficiency
6	育成(いくせい)する	bring up, promote
16	中味(なかみ)	substance, contents
	園芸(えんげい)	horticulture
	畜産(ちくさん)	livestock industry

〔p. 120〕

19	～ではコトがすまない	*idiom*, it is not enough to～

〔p. 121〕

2	抑える	restrain, control
3	農業基本法	basic laws of agriculture
4	助長する	promote, foster
5	GHQ	General Headquarters of the Supreme Command of the Allied Powers
8	そこへもってきて	*idiom*, in addition to that
10	バクチをはる	gamble
11	当る	hit, turn out well, succeed
	なきゃあ	*colloq.*, ＝なければ
12	覚悟	readiness, resignation
	バラバラの	scattering, sporadic [onomatopoeic word]
14	タイミング	timing
15	法人	corporation
16	いったって	*colloq.*, ＝いっても
18	亡霊	ghost, departed soul, apparition
	さまよう	wander about, rove
19	自然発生的に	spontaneously
22	愛知県	Aichi prefecture
	請負	contract, contracted work
23	やってやる	＝してあげる

〔p. 122〕

1	単位で	as a unit
8	委託する	entrust

〔p. 122〕

9	離脱(りだつ)する	break away from, leave
13	表彰(ひょうしょう)する	commend, honor, make public recognition of
15	笠(りゅう)　信太郎(しんたろう)	1900–1967, 朝日新聞論説委員長(あさひしんぶんろんせついいんちょう)
16	論説委員(ろんせついいん)	editorial writer
17	裏打(うらう)ちする	back
18	試行錯誤(しこうさくご)	trial and error
20	定着(ていちゃく)する	take root, fix

〔p. 123〕

2	診断(しんだん)	diagnosis
3	融和(ゆうわ)	harmony, reconciliation
4	条項(じょうこう)	condition, term
10	タイプ	type
	値(あた)いする	be worthy of～. ～に値いする
13	田(た)んぼ	rice field, paddy
14	水(みず)かけ	watering (a field)
	刈取(かりと)り	reaping, a harvest
18	分配(ぶんぱい)	distribution, sharing
20	田植(たう)え	rice planting
21	なんにもせんのも、いましょうね	*colloq.*, ＝なんにもしない人もいるでしょうね
23	えらい	great, phenomenal

〔p. 124〕

4	土地所有権絶対(とちしょゆうけんぜったい)	absoluteness of land ownership
7	折角(せっかく)の	special
9	知恵(ちえ)	wisdom, brains
10	乗(の)り切(き)る	ride through, get over (difficulties)

〔p. 124〕

13	エライ	great
14	おもったって	*colloq.*, ＝おもっても
	弁舌（べんぜつ）さわやかに	eloquently, fluently
15	強引（ごういん）に	forcibly, in a high-handed manner
16	まあいける	*colloq.*, that's good, that may do
20	合作社（がつさくしや）	cooperative firm [in China]
	ノルマ	norm [from Russian, 'norma']
21	ボーナス	bonus
23	なまける	be idle, be lazy

〔p. 125〕

6	モラル	moral
9	システム	system
12	計理（けいり）	accounting
13	株式会社（かぶしきがいしや）	joint-stock corporation
14	利益分配（りえきぶんぱい）	profit sharing
20	太陽光線（たいようこうせん）	sunlight
21	永久不変（えいきゆうふへん）の	everlasting

〔p. 126〕

4	やれなんだ	*colloq.*, and so on, and so forth
7	しれている	be negligible, be obvious
	減反（げんたん）	reduction of farmland
9	住宅敷地（じゆうたくしきち）	residential site, lot, tract housing
	想定（そうてい）する	suppose
13	かりに～としても	for example
17	養鶏（ようけい）	poultry farm

〔p. 126〕

21	加工業(かこうぎょう)	processing industry
22	鶏(にわとり)	chicken
	豚(ぶた)	pig
	エサ(餌)	feed
	玉子(たまご)	(chicken) egg

〔p. 127〕

6	資本投下(しほんとうか)	capital investment
7	米作麦作(べいさくばくさく)	rice and barley farming
	菜作(さいさく)	vegetable growing
8	果樹作(かじゅさく)	fruit growing
	酪農(らくのう)	dairy farming
15	鹿児島県(かごしまけん)	Kagoshima prefecture
	ジャパン・ファーム	Japan Farm
16	三菱(みつびし)	Mitsubishi (financial clique)
	～羽(わ)	counter for 'bird'
17	～もの	as many as ～, as much as ～
	農林中金(のうりんちゅうきん)	＝農林中央金庫(のうりんちゅうおうきんこ), Agriculture and Forestry Bank
20	投入(とうにゅう)する	invest, throw into
22	ブロイラー	broiler (chicken)
	需給(じゅきゅう)	supply and demand
23	役立(やくだ)つ	be useful, be effective
	間接的(かんせつてき)に	indirectly

〔p. 128〕

3	処理加工(しょりかこう)	processing
4	太刀打(たちう)ちする	compete, cross swords
7	足(あし)を引(ひ)っぱる	hinder, harm
9	基調(きちょう)	basis, keynote

〔p. 128〕

11	やたらに	indiscriminately
14	何(なん)ぞや	*literary*, ＝何であろうか
15	新鮮(しんせん)な	fresh
	混(ま)ぜもの	mixture, filler, foreign matter
	バタ	butter
	チーズ	cheese
16	ハム	ham
	ソーセージ	sausage
17	開発(かいはつ)する	cultivate, develop (resources)
22	自給自足(じきゅうじそく)	self-sufficiency

〔p. 129〕

1	一億(いちおく)	one hundred million
7	世界連邦(せかいれんぽう)	united world
13	いらん	＝いらない
15	原料(げんりょう)	raw materials
19	ペタペタ	＝ペコペコ, servilely, cringingly [onomatopoeic word used as an adverb]
22	相互流通(そうごりゅうつう)	mutual circulation

〔p. 130〕

11	ああいう	＝あのような
17	～せい	＝～せよ，～しろ，～しなさい [dialectal form of the imperative ～せよ]
23	国境付近(こっきょうふきん)に	near national boundaries
	過疎(かそ)	sparseness

〔p. 131〕

1	温存(おんぞん)する	preserve

〔p. 131〕

2	レクリエーション	recreation
4	一朝非常時（いっちょうひじょうじ）	emergency
5	鍬（くわ）	hoe
6	ドル・ショック	"dollar shock"
	騒（さわ）ぐ	be alarmed, be agitated
11	知（し）ってます	＝知っています
13	ジャーナリスト	journalist
	わいわい	vehemently [onomatopoeic word]
16	サラリーマン	salaried man
17	鋭（するど）い	shrewd, keen, sharp
20	真剣（しんけん）	serious, earnest
21	余計（よけい）なお世話（せわ）	unsolicited advice
22	ヒマな	unoccupied

〔p. 132〕

4	逆手（ぎゃくて）	dirty trick
6	根強（ねづよ）い	firmly-rooted
8	暮（くら）しの手帖（てちょう）	a quarterly home journal
	団野（だんの）　信夫（のぶお）	1909–，ジャーナリスト，元朝日新聞社監査役（かんさやく）

19　日本語のテンス

〔p. 133〕

2	動詞（どうし）	verb
	テンス	tense [grammatical term]
4	複雑（ふくざつ）きわまる	extremely complicated
5	人称（にんしょう）	person [grammatical term]
	ムード	mood [grammatical term]
6	私（わたくし）ども	＝私など
8	無造作（むぞうさ）な	simple and easy, artless
	単純（たんじゅん）な	simple
11	ジャンケン〔ポン〕	toss up. *literally*, play the game 'rock, scissors, paper'
14	不精密（ふせいみつ）な	imprecise, inaccurate

〔p. 134〕

1	比（くら）べる	compare with
5	現在（げんざい）	the present tense
	未来（みらい）	the future tense
	過去（かこ）	the past tense
9	過去完了（かこかんりょう）	the past perfect tense
11	落（お）とす	drop, lose
	がまぐち	purse
	拾（ひろ）う	pick up
19	有能（ゆうのう）	able, capable
21	助動詞（じょどうし）	auxiliary verb
22	言（い）い切（き）りの形（かたち）	sentence final form
	連用形（れんようけい）	continuative form, conjuga-

〔p. 134〕

		tional form

〔p. 135〕

3	センテンス	sentence
5	意地悪(いじわる)い	ill-tempered, cross
	かつぐ	play a trick, deceive
6	家内(かない)	(my) wife
	新宿(しんじゅく)	place-name, a district in Tokyo
	寄(よ)る	stop at
8	伊勢丹(いせたん)	a name of a department store
	エレベーター	elevator
11	うっかり	carelessly, absentmindedly
	ひっくり返(かえ)す	turn over
16	何階(なんがい)	some floor
20	ものが言(い)える	be able to talk, be able to express
21	金田一(きんだいち)　春彦(はるひこ)	1913–, 国語学,　東京外国語大学, 東京芸術大学講師

20　れる・られる

〔p. 136〕

2	自発（じはつ）	spontaneity
4	開業医（かいぎょうい）	medical practitioner
	診断書（しんだんしょ）	medical report
5	向う（むこう）	next
6	安静加療（あんせいかりょう）	rest and medical care
8	法廷（ほうてい）	court (of law)
9	あるなし	be or not to be
	微妙（びみょう）な	delicate, subtle
11	治療（ちりょう）	medical treatment
13	引（ひ）っ込（こ）みのつかない	go too far to retreat, be unable to back out
15	治癒（ちゆ）する	treat, cure
	多寡（たか）	＝多（おお）いか少（すく）ないか, number, quantity, amount
18	主（ぬし）	person, master

〔p. 137〕

1	含（ふく）み	implication
2	しょい込（こ）む	burden oneself with, carry on one's back
4	恩師（おんし）	a teacher who has not only taught one but has taken an interest in one's personal affairs
8	運勢判断（うんせいはんだん）	reading of one's fortune

〔p. 137〕

8	～にせよ～にせよ	[one chooses a few examples and indicates that they are not exceptions to what is stated in the main sentence] take～ or～for example
9	万人（ばんにん）	everybody
10	～に至（いた）っては	[an expression used to focus on an extreme case] as for～
11	目前（もくぜん）に迫（せま）る	be close at hand, be imminent
12	コンピューター	computer
14	世人（せじん）	people, the world, the public
	誤差（ごさ）	error
	追求（ついきゅう）する	pursue, follow after, seek after
15	まして	S_1.～S_2 [one picks out a specific case (i.e., 医師の診断書) from the preceding sentence and shows that even to that case something (i.e., 厳しい誤差の追求) does not apply; therefore, it is not likely that the same thing (i.e., 厳しい誤差の追求) applies to a minor case (i.e., られるのあるなし)] much less～
21	個人差（こじんさ）	difference (*or* variation) among individuals
22	有無（うむ）	＝あるかないか, existence, presence

	〔p. 137〕	
22	吟味(ぎんみ)する	examine closely
	〔p. 138〕	
2	人柄(ひとがら)	personality, character
4	退化(たいか)する	degenerate, retrograde
5	とり組(く)む	wrestle with, face. 〜にとり組む
6	よみがえる	be brought back to life, be freshened
7	奥(おく)ゆかしさ	refined, courtly, graceful
8	責任(せきにん)のがれ	avoidance of responsibility
10	普遍妥当性(ふへんだとうせい)	universal validity
11	あやぶまれる	be doubtful
12	軽率(けいそつ)に	carelessly, hastily, rashly
	ひかえ目(め)	moderate, reserved
13	不用意(ふようい)に	carelessly
14	恥(はじ)をかく	disgrace oneself, be put to shame
	予防線(よぼうせん)	prevention, protection
15	使(つか)いこなす	master (a skill), acquire command of
17	いちいち	fully, in full
19	うるさく	annoyingly, persistently
20	素(そ)っ気(け)なく	brusquely, curtly, bluntly
	〔p. 139〕	
5	難事(なんじ)	difficult matter, trouble
6	受身(うけみ)	passive
	可能(かのう)	potential
	尊敬(そんけい)	honorific
7	ことごとく	all

〔p. 139〕

7	通覧(つうらん)する	survey, look over
8	名(な)の通(とお)った	renowned, famous
10	試(ため)す	try, experiment
11	聞(き)きただす	confirm, verify, ascertain
15	見過(みすご)す	overlook, pass over, escape one's notice
18	きめのこまかい	extremely careful, fine
20	サンスクリット	Sanskrit
	ギリシア	Greek
	ラテン	Latin
	中動相(ちゅうどうそう)	the middle voice
22	能動(のうどう)	the active voice
	相(そう)	voice, aspect

〔p. 140〕

1	山下(やました)　正男(まさお)	a person's name
7	埋没(まいぼつ)する	be (*or* lie) buried
8	露(つゆ)	dew
10	万葉集(まんようしゅう)	a 20-volume anthology of poetry compiled in the 8th century
	山上(やまのうえの)　憶良(おくら)	660–733?, poet
11	瓜(うり)	melon
	食(は)めば	*classical*, ＝食(た)べれば
	思(おも)ほゆ	*classical*, ＝思われる
	栗(くり)	chestnut
	偲(しの)ばゆ	*classical*, ＝偲ばれる，思い出(だ)される
	何処(いずこ)より	*classical and literary*, ＝どこから
12	眼交(まなかい)に	*classical*, ＝目の前に

〔p. 140〕

12	もとな	*classical*, ＝しきりに
	懸(かか)りて	*classical and literary*,＝かかって, hang
	安眠(やすい)	*classical*, ＝安眠(あんみん), quiet sleep
16	ちらつく	flicker, be haunted by
18	発話者(はつわしや)	speaker
20	夢想(むそう)	dream, a day dream
21	和歌(わか)	31-syllable poem
	発句(ほつく)	17-syllable poem, an early form of haiku
22	脳(のう)	brain

〔p. 141〕

1	神秘的(しんぴてき)	mystical, miraculous
	授(さず)ける	grant, award
4	夢十夜(ゆめじゆうや)	title of a collection of short stories, *Ten Nights' Dreams*
	運慶(うんけい)	?–1223, sculptor
5	護国寺(ごこくじ)	a name of a temple
	仁王(におう)	the two Buddhist guardian kings sculpted in fierce postures and often seen at temple entrances
	彫(ほ)る	carve, sculpt
6	のみ	chisel
7	つち	hammer
8	ストーリー	story, plot
11	西洋(せいよう)だね	Western source
12	ダ・ヴィンチ	Leonardo da Vinci

〔p. 141〕

15	コントロールがきく	bring under control
	井伏(いぶせ) 鱒二(ますじ)	1898–, 小説家
16	さざなみ軍記(ぐんき)	book title, *War Diary of a Young General* (a modern novel about the 12th century Gempei War)
	美少年(びしょうねん)	handsome youth
17	ユーモア	humor
	告白(こくはく)する	confess
19	境地(きょうち)	stage one has attained through experience
	無我忘我(むがぼうが)	selflessness and self-oblivion
	美談(びだん)	praiseworthy (*or* instructive) anecdote
	語(かた)り草(ぐさ)	topic, topic on everyone's lips
20	範疇(はんちゅう)	category
21	夢殿(ゆめどの)	name of an octogonal pavilion at Japan's oldest temple, Hōryūji, built in 739
	救世観音(ぐぜかんのん)	name of a statue of the Bodhisattva Kannon
22	志賀(しが) 直哉(なおや)	1883–1972, 小説家

〔p. 142〕

3	浮(うか)ぶ	come across one's mind
4	遊離(ゆうり)する	isolate, separate
	格別(かくべつ)な	＝特別(とくべつ)な
5	若(も)し	＝もし
6	冠(かん)する	crown

〔p. 142〕

8	気(き)にかける	＝気にする
9	箇所(かしょ)	＝ところ, line
10	破目(はめ)	difficult situation, dilemma
16	けじめ	distinction, difference
17	恬然(てんぜん)として	indifferently, brazenly
	手合(てあい)	people, fellow
18	ごろごろする	＝あちこちにいる
	当節(とうせつ)	＝今頃(いまごろ)
19	であって見(み)れば	if it would be so
22	暗夜行路(あんやこうろ)	book title, *The Road of the Dark Night* (a novel)
	蝮(まむし)のお政(まさ)	"Viper" Omasa, a character's name
23	くだり	passage

〔p. 143〕

1	懺悔(ざんげ)	penitence, contrition
	～こつきり	＝～こっきり ＝ ～かぎり, just (once), exactly (once)
3	興行(こうぎょう)する	give (a performance), run (a show)
7	人為的(じんいてき)	artificial, unnatural
8	しくむ	contrive, plan, plot
9	そらぞらしい	palpable, obvious, empty
	偽(いつわ)り	lie, falsehood
	所業(しょぎょう)	action, deed
12	作為(さくい)	artificiality
14	好悪(こうお)	one's likes and dislikes, partiality, preference

〔p. 143〕

14	直様(すぐさま)	＝直(す)ぐ, at once, directly
15	此方(こちら)	this side, I, we
18	検証(けんしょう)	verification, inspection
21	ぎこちない	awkward, clumsy
22	捉(とら)へられる	＝捉えられる, be caught (by the idea)
	しっくり	exactly, to a "T," in tune

〔p. 144〕

3	本居(もとおり)　宣長(のりなが)	1730–1801, 国学者
	物(もの)のあはれ	fine sensibility
4	范(はん)の犯罪(はんざい)	book title, *The Crimes of Han* (a novel)
6	詞華集(しかしゅう)	anthology
	とんでもない	absurd, inconceivable
	誤訳(ごやく)	mistranslation
7	中野(なかの)　好夫(よしお)	1903–, 英文(えいぶん)学, 評論家
11	適宜(てきぎ)	according to circumstances, fittingly
15	どうかすると	in some way or other
	鐘(かね)	bell, gong
	鳴(な)る	ring, toll
	撞木(しゅもく)	wooden hammer
16	禅問答(ぜんもんどう)	questions and answers in a Zen ritual
	～めく	[N＋めく] look (like), have an air of～
19	板坂(いたさか)　元(げん)	1922–, 江戸文学, 元ハーバード大学講師

さくいん

This is an index to all vocabulary and notes with the exception of names of persons. Numbers refer to the page and line numbers carried at the outer margin of the text pages.